Praise for
LOSS TO LEGACY: A STEPPING ST(
TO HEALING AND TRANSFORN

"This work is an amazing contribution to grief literature. It will help you reach new insights and understanding about your grief journey. Beautiful writing, beautiful story telling. The depth of Lily's experiences shines through in every aspect of this wonderful book. Read it, breathe in what you learn from the stories, and work the exercises step by step. You will be transformed in ways you've never imagined."

—Julie Lockhart, retired Executive Director of WinterSpring Center: Facing Loss, Embracing Life Again

"From the author of *Two Rare Birds: A Legacy of Love* comes a new book that offers readers a step-by-step guide to navigating life-shattering loss toward life-affirming healing. In a society that insists we "move on" from sorrow, Lily invites us instead to dive deeply into it, to discover our own unique story and embrace its transformative power. Read this book. No matter the nature of your grief, it will give you courage, strength, and a path for thinking and acting differently about life, death, and love."

—Martha Kay (MK) Nelson Director of Psycho-Social Care, Mission Hospice & Home Care

"Lily Myers Kaplan has written a deep and moving guide to finding our way through sorrow and creating a legacy to honor those we've lost. With wisdom and grace, she has led us through the early days of profound grief and forward into meaning and action. No matter whether your loss is recent or not so recent, her wonderful book, *Loss to Legacy*, belongs on your shelf and in your heart."

—Cheryl Jones, host of Voice America Radio's *Good Grief*, grief counselor, and author of the novel, *An Ocean Between Them*

"Lily Myers Kaplan has done a fantastic job of putting her body of work into a deep, rich and accessible form. As I followed the path Lily generously offers, I was able to transform my waves of inconsolable grief around species death, declining planetary health, and many personal losses...all at my own pace. I'm deeply changed by walking these stepping stones and am inspired to reframe loss into love, honor and grace. I heartily recommend Loss to Legacy to anyone who grieves."

—Dean Walker, author of *The Impossible Conversation* and founder of Living Resilience

"Lily Myers Kaplan is a wise storyteller who has learned the depths of grief and resurrection the hard way and she offers her hard-won wisdom to the rest of us. Her book is a stunning testament to the heart of being human and the personal transformation possible when one grieves deeply and well."

–Carolyn North, author of *The Experience of a Lifetime: Living Fully, Dying Consciously*

"Lily Kaplan's *Loss to Legacy* is a beautiful, unique guide to dealing with loss and grief. It vastly expands our cultural understandings of grief, from something to be moved through as fast as possible to showing how our inevitable losses are embedded with the potential for discovering ones purpose and wholeness. *Loss to Legacy* reveals how life-defining legacies for future generations can emerge from loss. Weaving together profound concepts with poignant stories and a comprehensive set of exercises for turning the pain of grief into a pathway of transformation, *Loss to Legacy* touched me deeply. I recommend it wholeheartedly."

–Ron Pevny, founding director of the Center for Conscious Eldering
and author of *Conscious Living, Conscious Aging*

"*Loss to Legacy* will take you safely and surely through a process from your own healing depths into an utterly new life. With Lily's wise guidance, be ready to dive deep, surface transformed, and move into who you are and what your life is calling you to do."

–Shoshana Alexander, Playwright/creator of *Taking Our Life,* a stage play about suicide, ecocide and daring to live. Co-author of *Awakening Joy: 10 Steps to Happiness*

LOSS TO LEGACY

Maggie,

May your legacy
shine through your
grief. Lily

LOSS TO LEGACY

A stepping stone path to healing and transformation

LILY MYERS KAPLAN

Rainbow Bridge Press
Applegate, Oregon

Rainbow Bridge Press
c/o Spirit of Resh Foundation
PO Box 1119
Jacksonville, OR 97530
www.reshfoundation.org

ISBN: 978-0-692-52998-0

Printed in the United States of America

Don't run away from grief, o soul,
Look for the remedy inside the pain,
because the rose came from the thorn
and the ruby came from a stone.

–Rumi

CONTENTS

WELCOME

Dear Readers,

Imagine the possibility that your story of loss, grief, and sorrow can be rewritten until it becomes completely new, building on the old as a foundation for everything yet to come. Imagine, as in the alchemy of the ancients, turning the lead of your sorrows into the gold of a legacy built from your renewed story of meaning and renovated life purpose. This book is a guide to that possibility. Grounded in an archetypal pattern of transformation, your story will become the foundation of eight Stepping Stones, paving a trail that has helped countless grievers through the mire of mourning. These Stepping Stones take you on a wander through your own grief and loss, elicit reflections, invite vision, and develop actions that help you carve your very own footpath to healing.

This book is filled with my own stories of grief, loss, renewal, and restoration after three of my beloveds died within one year. I traveled to the depths of a down-to-my-knees, grief-stricken self. I unraveled my sense of belonging to the world, then rewove myself back into revitalized passion, purpose, and capacity to appreciate the preciousness of Life. If I could do that, so can you. My losses were the catalyst that led me down a road of learning more about myself than I ever expected. I mined the depths of my sorrows as I replayed the stories of my family, their lives and deaths, their values and attributes, and all the ways we hurt and helped one another. I explored the twists and turns of relationships and cultivated appreciation for the direct correlation between my aching heart and my undying love. I accepted the beauty of being wounded as part and parcel of the whole human experience. I grew to value my humanity and theirs, with all our flaws and strengths rolled into one beautiful package. And I uncovered the greatest gift of all: the ability to hurt without suffering.

When loss comes through illness, death of a beloved, job change, relationship ending, cultural and planetary degradation, or stage of life, your known and relied-upon identity can be a casualty, leaving you no longer feeling like the real you. Yet true healing (not fixing, covering, or denying) is possible. I imagine you thinking, *Yes . . . but how?* My response is this: *you can traverse this tumultuous territory by bravely, step by step, following a map.* The stories in this book, both mine and others, guide you through that map.

Finding your way through loss, in whatever form it has arrived, through this Stepping Stone process, is a path that relies on a wholehearted embrace of your own story. It requires steadfast determination. In a culture that doesn't readily accept death and emphatically sweeps grief under the rug, you will need to overcome the cultural forces demanding that strong emotions be kept hidden. Courage, daring, and dedication, will be, and must be, your faithful and trusted companions if you are to conquer the prevalent but unspoken message to *Move on!* We deeply feel this subtle, and sometimes glaring, burying of grief. Human resource departments with three-day bereavement policies and kindly neighbors with well-intended platitudes of support often miss the mark. Grief with all its messiness becomes a private affair, left unmet and unwitnessed. We desperately need the communal source of sustenance that comes from being witnessed in our pain. We cannot heal alone.

By bucking this system and inviting death and its accompanying loss to be your teacher, you can recover your inner spark. I certainly found this to be true. When I went beyond cultural norms in order to feel my anguish, those very feelings became the primal matter that awakened insights about the purpose of life and its handmaiden, death. This led me to my own reason for living. How do *you*, amid this cultural overlay, allow authentic grief and full-hearted mourning? Willingness, tenacity, and skill building are keys that unlock your door. Together they open the possibility of being remolded into a new, forever-changed form.

The stories and Stepping Stones in this book, with their twists, turns, and profound authenticity, connect us in our shared grief. They are guiding lights on the path to that courageous, tenacious skill building. Stories about loss and death are great equalizers. They bring us together, regardless of heritage, ethnic background, life circumstances, or political affiliations. As they pave the trail, the stories encourage you to take heart, reminding you that, although your grief is your own, you are not alone. While some names have been changed to protect privacy, every story in this book is true.

Loss to Legacy workshop participants have nobly and resolutely followed these Stepping Stones until reaching the center of the labyrinth. They report finding meaning amid suffering, more ease in the ebb and flow of sorrow, increased freedom from cultural constraints, and, most potent of all, a clear mission grown from the losses they've encountered. The Stones ask for your readiness; they are for those of you willing to dig deep into your story of loss. They will steep you in symbolism and self-inquiry until you've winnowed every bit of marrow from the bones of your sorrow. For some of you, they may be premature. If you are stunned with raw, untenable grief, it would be a soul violation to bypass your feelings with meaning-making. I would not do that to you. For you, who are in the deepest lament of your lives, I suggest that you wait. You may find solace in simply reading the stories; then take the steps slowly when the time is right. Either way, the path is always here, awaiting your first step when you are ready. Trust yourself.

If you feel a just-before-you-step-on-a-roller-coaster belly-drop or a big *Yes!* or a tentative hope, then it's time to grab your hat, lace up your boots, and step onto the winding footpath of transformative grieving. The trail is just a few paces in front of you. I welcome you onto it. Wherever and whenever you begin, and however you choose to journey through this process, you are invited to enter a new relationship with your mourning, transforming your loss into a legacy that makes a difference. May it be so!

Warmly,

Section One

MOURNING TO MEANING

Chapter One
MY YEAR OF DEATH

My deep encounter with death through loss of my most intimates didn't visit until I was well into my fifties. Before then, people I loved died and I lay on my bed, crying. But life-shattering loss, the kind that demolished me, came when I was fifty-seven and had already experienced both the blessing and curse of other kinds of loss—relationship endings and betrayals, career changes, and health challenges. I learned how to translate loss into meaning the hard way, getting an education through one dark night of the soul after another. These middle-of-the-night inquiries into what mattered, what had meaning for me, and what was *right action* were helpful when, all of a sudden, I entered a spinning vortex that pulled four of my immediate family members out of this world, gone in a flash. Dad went first. He was a bigger-than-life force of passion, creativity, and self-direction—a businessman who made his way in the world with brute determination and lionhearted loyalty to his own vision of success. When he decided to choose death over a feeding tube, we gathered 'round him in loving attention and quiet meditation. We fed him a last meal by hand. One strawberry, fully enjoyed. Ten days later he died in the aloneness of midnight, a fitting passage for a lover of Edgar Allen Poe's dark poetry.

Mom's death a couple years later was accompanied by a slow deterioration into Alzheimer's disease. "This is not Mom," my sisters and I reminded each other when her graceful countenance turned into stubborn belligerence. She became a woman who couldn't remember how to walk, string words into sentences, or feed herself. I grieved for her long before her body gave out, often crying after a phone call during which she spoke only gibberish. When she died quietly and suddenly, taken by a heart attack, we were relieved. Yet tears still streamed down our cheeks as we gathered, virtually, since we were scattered from East Coast to West. My eldest sister, Sally, sat by Mom's Maryland nursing home bedside and held a cell phone aloft as we wished her spirit a loving goodbye. Just three months later, when Lois, my not-quite-fifty-nine-year-old sister, died, I was knocked to my knees. Though I'd sat in vigil five times over thirteen years, as a scalpel carved cancerous cells from her brain, I still wasn't ready for the destined outcome when it came. Nine months after that, Lois's husband, Dave, died from colorectal cancer. They shared a fourteen-year in-tandem cancer journey that was a neverending stream of double whammies and traumatic slam-bam-no-thank-you-ma'am treatments and surgeries.

My family of origin was reduced from five to four; then suddenly, there were only two of us left. Three beloveds died in a one-year cycle, and four in just under two. My still-living-and-breathing sister, Sally, calls this our *Year of Death*. And while it was the most profoundly troubling and difficult period of my life, I recall the sad memories within a soft golden glow, much like the movie imagery of a dream. Traumatic, yes. Debilitating, definitely. But more than that? Absolutely! I shared this whole story in my memoir, *Two Rare Birds: A Legacy of Love*, recounting my journey from belly-wrenching sobs and lost sense of self to finding and recovering gifts hidden in the swamp of my sorrow. I took my readers with me along a meandering path through the underworld of my soul. And they witnessed my climb back to the land of the living with renewed meaning and purpose. Here's an excerpt from *Two Rare Birds*, where my journey began:

With Lois gone, the foundation of who I knew myself to be was yanked from under my feet, dropping me right down to my knees, where I stayed for an entire year. Months after her passing, on my one day of freedom from the demands of directing Oakland Feather River Family Camp,

I'd suddenly descend into sheer wailing, as if on cue. Driving through wildflower laden, rushing snow-melt-filled mountain passes, my car, a bubble of deepest privacy, is where my grief found its most holy expression. The rainbow-colored basket into which I'd nestled the tiny stuffed bear with its lifelike, movable arms and legs—one of Lo's prized possessions—hung from the rear-view mirror. It bounced down the country roads with me as I mourned my sister and my lost self. Among the balsam scent of 150-foot pines, tucked on a sunny spit of sand beside a crystal mountain lake, I cried and ranted and slept, and let my heart break. *Who would I be in a world without a Lois in it?* I wondered. I had no idea.

My process included discovering how Lois and Dave's grace and appreciation for life, with all its laughter and tears amid their diseases, taught me about forgiveness and that love is what matters most. I honed my hard-won wisdom until it centered on a fresh perspective toward the beauty of being alive. It evolved into certainty that a relationship with death influences how we choose to live. The day Lois's doctors declared her terminal, with just weeks to live, I walked the streets near my downtown Oakland, California, office. I saw mothers and toddlers, teens on bikes, and businessmen at coffee shops. In my daze, unbidden thoughts came: *that person is going to die.* Then, *that little boy is going to die one day, too.* Over and over I saw the mortality of each human before me, no matter the age. And the big realization *I will die, too!* hit me in the gut. In a visceral, deep-knowing kind of way, I acknowledged then accepted the certainty of my own death. I prepared to say goodbye to Lois with a newfound, albeit uninvited, recognition of the truth of her oft-repeated words: *this moment is all we have.* With Sally and Dave, I tended Lois during her final month of living with a profoundly life-altering understanding of how short and precious life is. While my year of death produced a crippling and dismantling grief accompanied by a stunning loss of identity, two years later I found myself in the throes of a burgeoning new sense of Self and life direction. That's where *Two Rare Birds* ended—at my new beginning:

My losses have led me to accept that being born, living a life, and facing death are parts of one whole package. And the truth of what Lois said again and again, "This moment is all we have," is finally emblazoned permanently in my heart. Death, in all its terrible, heart-cracking, life-shattering ways has shown me that any day could be the last. No longer will I wait to love, to forgive, or to walk, as best I can, in beauty. The realization that none of us will escape death became more real than ever. Losing Lois and Dave had broken through my denial of mortality. It dawned on me that hiding death represses the heart and I felt a growing passion to bring it out of the closet. Spirit of Resh Foundation is my legacy in progress, born from the love of my Ancestors. It is the sweet fruit of my Tree of Life, and my awakening into a wholly—and holy—renewed purpose for living.

My navigation through that passage is the foundation of this Stepping Stone path from loss to legacy. My own stories illuminate the trail—one that you will undertake later in this book. At first, I was groping through the darkness, sinking underwater, and struggling to breathe. But my earlier years of training through the school of hard knocks, learning-the-hard-way to find meaning in life's challenges, took hold. Years earlier, I'd turned the tumultuous ending of a meaningful career, and its devastating loss of identity, into renewed purpose. I started a SoulWorks counseling practice, helping people find their most authentic selves. I knew I could reinvent myself again. When Lois died, I called upon the same principles I applied back then, excavating my emotions in order to mine the buried treasures of my soul. Combined with journaling, engaging in nature, and opening to mythic and symbolic awareness, I put myself back together. There were times when all I could do was sit still. Or I could barely sit at all. Other times I crawled, clawing my way toward meaning. But through all of it, I wandered through days that turned into months, then years, with a deep appreciation for the gift of Life. My heart swelled with gratitude for my family's lives entwined with mine.

Once, when I literally dragged myself along a rocky river shoreline, I thought of the Mary Oliver poem "Wild Geese." She speaks of repentance, love, and despair. She says you don't have to crawl, but instead, to let your soft animal body love what it loves. She says that sharing your pain and listening to others' pain in return, is healing. I took her words to heart. I told the rocks, the river, and anyone who would listen about my sorrows, hoping that they'd hear me with their hearts. Yes, I crawled. Then I walked. Then I strode forward on two strong legs, grateful for the gifts Lois, Dave, and my parents gave me. I integrated the lessons I'd learned from their lives *and* their deaths: Remember love. Revere life. Accept challenges. Use everything to grow. This is their legacy to me. And mine to carry forward.

When I speak of legacy, I mean the totality of attitudes, values, and ethics that have been passed on, wittingly and unwittingly, by the people I've loved. Whether they are of my bloodline or not, once no longer embodied they are my Ancestors. This approach to ancestral legacy comes from an Indigenous Peoples way of seeing life and death. Around the world, earth-centered cultures honor the Ancestors (capitalized to signify honor) as the creators of life. They are fed ceremonially—both daily and on special holidays or occasions. Ancestors are an archetypal collection of forces: friends, community members, even beloved public figures who have left this life. I imagine their spirits living on in the hearts of those who cherish their names. Those whose names are no longer known also feed this invisible web of ancestral potency. The earth and cosmos, from which humans evolved, alongside the flora and fauna that inhabit this planet, are, for me, Ancestors. I appreciate the Indigenous Peoples perspective of adopting all life forms as Ancestors dancing, playing, and influencing our lives from the other side of a veil that separates this world from a vibrant yet invisible one. I wholeheartedly respect every human being's right to their own interpretation of the presence or absence of an afterlife and offer my personal concepts of legacy and Ancestors since they appear many times in the unfolding of these stories and Stepping Stones.

While my deeply rooted beliefs about the ancestral lands are helpful and healing, my wish that Lois and Dave hadn't been taken from life so early makes me ache for them at times. But it would be false to say that I'm not equally grateful for the transformation their deaths have stirred in me and their contribution to my unexpected but deeply needed healing. It's a legacy I don't want to give back. Those life-changing lessons are like shimmering gems brought from my depths into the light. And since giving them back isn't an option, sharing my path with the intention of supporting you to find the gold of your living legacies is the next best thing. I believe this mission makes my Ancestors smile.

Chapter Two
EARTH CYCLES:
LIFE, DEATH, AND REBIRTH

From the moment we are born, we are changing. We grow from an infant to a toddler, from a toddler to a child, and then into the powerful stage of transformation many parents dread—adolescence! Each developmental stage has challenges and pitfalls, as well as triumphs and accomplishments. Yet from a successful passage through adolescence comes a healthy young adult who will eventually die from that stage and be reborn into an accomplished maturity. Loss, in the form of metaphorical death, visits again and again. Each life stage is a loss followed by a gain. The frolicking fun of one's twenties dies, and for many of us the satisfaction of accomplished career projects or marriage and family is born in one's thirties and forties. Middle-aged fulfillment translates into wizened elderhood, continuing the cycle of growth and transformation all the way to death. Loss visits along the way—leaving home, graduation, job changes, illness, empty nests, divorce, death of beloveds, or moving from one state or country to another. Learning to navigate these passages and losses is to recognize and accept them as a natural and necessary life, death, and rebirth cycle.

This is also nature's way, a never-ending cycling between seasons. As the earth spins its way through space, tilting toward the sun and then away, we call this a change of seasons. Increased light and warmth are followed by cold, deepened darkness. Spring, the season of birth and rebirth, follows winter, the season of death. Always. Summer's vitality is inevitably followed by autumn's decline until the cycle gives way to winter's death once again. It's the same for human beings. Like the planet, the inner psyche of humans circle around a never-ending wheel of inner seasons. Like a microcosm of our planetary cycles, these inner seasons mirror nature, and tracking them helps us navigate the ebb and flow of our confusing lives.

Imagine a wheel of life, death, and rebirth that maps earth seasons alongside the seasons of the human psyche. On the wheel, drawn from Indigenous wisdom, the four directions mark four seasons of inner and outer life. There is no beginning and no end to the wheel. We circle our way around it, revisiting the seasons of life in our own psychic pattern. Spring lies in the east of the wheel, where the sun rises, bringing new beginnings. It's where our relationship with a loved one, career, or other parts of life we may have lost began. Inner spring is a time of rebirth. Summer, the southern point of the wheel, is high noon. This is the time of greatest passion and life expression. It's where the fullness of our relationship with our beloved (in any form) resides. Autumn, the place of sunset, stands in the western section of the wheel. Our inner autumn is a period of deep introspection. We sift and sort through unresolved emotions or callings in the autumn of our inner world. This is where we unravel our story of loss and prepare for the descent ahead. The north marker on the wheel is winter, akin to the darkest hour of night. As a symbolic death it's a long, dark night of the soul. It's where we choose to allow our complete dismantling. Where our humbling grief resides. An internal winter, like the earth season it mirrors, eventually gives way to spring. Always. This knowledge suggests acceptance and patience. Wherever we are on the wheel, we must trust that it revolves from one season to the next, and with it, so do we. Despite appearances, the winter of a descent-into-grief will not last forever.

In ancient times, people of earth-based cultures knew this and celebrated each season; all cycles of life, death, and rebirth were recognized and honored. While there are pockets of people who still celebrate the passing seasons, Western culture has mostly split away from a natural relationship with the earth and these inherent cycles. Add to that a modern medical approach designed to prolong life at all costs and advertising campaigns with anti-aging platitudes as the cultural norm, and the sum total is a society in denial of death. This denial strips us of our true inheritance from the earth: acceptance of loss, death, and grief as an inevitable part of life.

I knew that Lois was dying long before any medical professional said so. It was as if to recognize death would admit failure. To this day, I wonder how her final months would've been different if we'd collectively acknowledged this truth. Would she have gone through that fifth brain surgery? Lois's doctors surely knew that death was approaching as cancer cells spread across her brain. If they'd approached death with greater acceptance, would they have suggested hospice rather than one more surgery? Would she still have fallen from her walker, breaking her back, spending those last months of life in a tightly cinched, hip-to-armpit brace and in a wheelchair? The memories of decorating the hard, molded plastic that kept her upright but barely able to breathe bring me to deeper heartbreak than memories of her death. If the medical profession embraced dying as a natural part of life, would Lois have gone birding, her favorite pastime, at least once more before her final breath? We'll never know the answers, but in my heart of hearts, I'm confident she could have had more quality of life had we been better prepared for what was coming. If, culturally, we could sanction nature and its wheel of life, then would death and grief be treated with more respect? Would that make a difference for you? For a growing population of aging baby boomers headed toward the end? For our world? I believe it would.

Once we embrace death as a part of life, we realize the preciousness of being alive. We open to the imperative to respect life in every form: ourselves, humanity, and nature. The natural world is whole. Unlike the human mind, it cannot reflect upon itself. It is unsplit and unconflicted. When we connect with nature and the planetary earth body from which we humans are born, we are bridged to that wholeness. Since human beings are part of nature, made of the same essential matter as the earth, we are subject to the same cycles, including death. Admitting this helps us know that we are part of something larger than our brief human lives. This knowledge invites us to accept loss as an intrinsic and necessary part of who we are. It prepares us for death and its accompanying sorrow.

While our industrialized society denies death and masks the seasons, they can never be fully crushed. Bright green sprouts push through sidewalk cracks in spring. Crunchy leaves litter cement sidewalks each autumn. People emerge from high-rise apartments shedding the hibernation of winter just as regularly as farmers till the soil each spring. Wherever you live—city, town, or country—the signs of these natural cycles abound, inside yourself and outdoors. They are everywhere. To accept them brings cooperation with the reality of death and grief. Beyond changing how the medical profession approaches death and dying, this understanding would become the foundation of an inclusive respect for all people, places, and things. When the reality of life's impermanence sinks in, as it did for me when I walked the streets of Oakland, life's stunning beauty, in all forms and iterations, becomes transparent. Once the certainty of death breaks through denial, there is no person or life form that deserves anything less than respect, love, and honor. Wouldn't that mean that our oceans would be vitally alive instead of dying? Wouldn't diversity be welcome everywhere and all people finally, truly be treated equally? I believe it would.

This is how death and grief are great equalizers, leveling the playing field as they illuminate the magnificence of *all* living beings. Once that consciousness infiltrates society, I believe that communities and the individuals within them will care for one another along the whole spectrum of life, death, grief, and rebirth. Compassion will replace competition, and people will know how to be fearlessly present with one another through all the challenges of life, including aging, illness, death and grief.

THE UNDERWORLD

There are ancient mythologies that describe the human passage through these seasonal cycles, in much the same way that Shakespearean plays offer dramas that resonate with our own innermost selves. These archetypal tales offer guidance for the experience of being alive. The ancient Greek myth of two goddesses, Demeter and Persephone, is a transformational tale that explains the cyclical nature of existence. It describes the necessity and purpose of winter as the precursor to the emergence of spring. I first met the two goddesses in my early twenties. It was the first day of spring, the sky pressed down with gray winds and flurries of snow mixed with icy rain. Frank, the elder among my rag-tag crew of growers, landscapers, and horticulture therapists, called us together for a small ceremony welcoming the new season. We gathered in a steam-fogged greenhouse, standing on pebbly sand in muddy boots and plaid flannel shirts tucked into thick corduroy pants. We were guides for developmentally disabled clients who watered and weeded, fed and potted, then sold spring bedding plants to our community.

A dusky, late-afternoon sunlight filtered through panes of wavy glass as my companions and I stood, surrounded by dank, mossy undergrowth and long beds empty of potted plants. We raised glasses of beer clutched in bruised and blistered hands, our dirty fingernails an ode to our proud profession in which hands sunk into dark, rich soil and soaked in juicy, green chlorophyll. With beer as our sacred elixir held high, Frank intoned the mythical story of the ancient Greeks' passage of winter into spring.

He told us of the deep bond between these two goddesses—a mother and daughter named Demeter and Persephone—whose tale described vibrant earth turned into fallow land and back again. Falling into a sing-song cadence, Frank told the story of how the young Persephone was collecting narcissus in a sunlit meadow, out of sight of her mother, when the earth cracked open and Hades, King of the Underworld, burst forth and abducted Persephone into his earthy den. Filled with grief, Demeter, Goddess of the Grain, searched for her daughter to no avail. She grieved, then recoiled from the world until grain began to wither and the earth was laid bare. Winter, with its long, dark nights, brought scarcity and suffering. As the people cried out, Zeus, king of all the gods and goddesses, took pity on them. He ordered Hades to release Persephone. When mother and daughter were reunited, Demeter poured life into the earth, the grain was restored, and a new cycle of growth began. But Zeus, in his great wisdom, demanded one caveat. Persephone, no longer a maiden, was now Queen of the Underworld. She would be required to return to her husband, Hades, for three months each year. Zeus's decree ensured that every year winter would return as a necessary time of hibernation and seed renewal. And his wisdom equally ensured that her annual return would herald the coming of spring, a time of rebirth.

As Frank invoked the presence of spring, he said, "Today, let us welcome Persephone back. Let us greet her and celebrate this first day of spring with joy. We invite the spirit of renewed growth into our humble greenhouses. May abundance reign here again!" With that, we poured our grainy, fermented brew into the earth as a prayer for a bountiful season. We entered the rites of spring as growers of plants and supporters of souls. It was the first ceremony I experienced outside the religion of my birth, and I loved it. As I watched the earth drink the ale at our feet I thought, *I'm home.*

To say that our ritual celebration of Persephone and Demeter created the beauty and sweet-scented air of daffodils, tulips, and hyacinth that followed would be naive. But to say that this rich and vibrant ceremony awakened my sense of the cycles of life, and that my consciousness tapped into the wider and wilder mysteries of an archetypal, mythical world, is abundantly true. Demeter and Persephone taught me about death and rebirth in the greenhouses. As I wondered at the miracle of rebirth, I realized how inner life is mirrored by the earth. Demeter's grief was a winter in her heart *and* on the land. And it gave way to spring and a renewed, bountiful life. This renewal is possible for us all.

I found meaning in this myth during my time of cavernous grief. I reflected on how Persephone was initiated from maiden to queen during her time in the Underworld. If she could grow from being sequestered in this metaphorical underworld of death—a kind of deep surrender—then why not me, too? Could I find my way through the winter of my sorrow, into the spring of a new way of being? Could I surrender to my own dismantling? (Can you?) I began to consider the wisdom in archetypal stories and nature's cycles as a way to help me make sense of my life. When I found myself curled in a fetal position, wailing, I *knew* that no matter how dark my heart and deep my unknowing, Persephone, symbolizing the inevitability of spring, would rise in me again. Acting from this knowing was, and is, an act of courage, a necessity on a conscious mourning journey. The root of the word "courage" is from the Latin *cor*, meaning "heart." Facing death and grief is a path of the heart. It asks us to dive all the way in, with faith in our own eventual spring. I believe we can trust in the cycles and our inevitable renewal. This encourages us to accept the overwhelming darkness of our grief and to partner with that descent, knowing that in our own time we will emerge into the light through building a living legacy.

Chapter Three
DEATH AND GRIEF AS INITIATION

Fascinated by mythology and archetypal psychology, I convinced my graduate school professors to enroll me in an independent study program so I could study transformational myths. These myths exist for a reason. They illuminate difficult passages as opportunities for growth, change, and greater wholeness. Populated by gods, goddesses, otherworldly creatures, and humans grappling with issues of good and evil, power and victimization, life and death, myths reveal archetypal patterns, including the light and dark aspects of our entire existence. They teach us about the nature of life and why we're here.

The myth of Demeter and Persephone goes far beyond teaching us about the life, death, and rebirth cycles of the natural world. It shows us that death and grief are *initiations*—potent rites of passage that signify transformation. At the end of the story, when Demeter and Persephone reunite and spring returns, they are more than who they once were. More whole and more of who they are meant to be, they become keepers of the Elysian Mysteries, the transformational process of those undergoing a dark night of the soul. The myth reveals that when we recognize grief as a rite of passage buried beneath the layers of loss, we grow. Ancient storytellers knew that the process of initiation is hidden, much like the transmutation of seeds deep in the earth of winter. Demeter and Persephone's story reminds us that, while we can't see the process of transformation, it is happening in the mysterious unknown reaches of our innermost selves. While we flail and wail on the surface, endlessly searching for who or what no longer exists, we are being irrevocably re-formed beneath.

When Persephone was abducted, Demeter's grief, as it is for many of us whose beloveds have died, was all-encompassing. She searches so long and grieves so hard that her shimmering cloak becomes tattered and gray. Once vibrant, Demeter loses her goddess glow as she drags herself from forest to town in search of her lost daughter. Her true identity is gone. No one knows she is the great Demeter, Goddess of the Grain. This is much like our oh-so-human, real-life grief journey. Our true identity is missing, hidden even from ourselves, beneath our tattered gray cloak of devastation. As excruciating as it is, this wrenching dismemberment is a necessary part of the process if we are to be remade, initiated through the disintegration. The myth says that without dissolution, there is no transformation, no growing out of an old identity into a new one. Like Demeter, whose rage tears her apart, we experience our pain, anger, remorse, regret, and railing against the unfairness of loss as all-consuming. Identities and roles that once had meaning are shed like the skin of a snake until we no longer feel like ourselves. Demeter's long and arduous search is like our own. The futility of wishing life was different and lamenting our *if only's* brings the necessary unraveling of who we once were. This unwinding must happen before we are able to reweave ourselves into who and what we shall become.

The story explores every step of Demeter's grief journey, recounting her collapse at a well in the center of a village. It explains her sojourn there, tending to the village hearth. We're being shown this symbolic well as the center of our own being, from which all nourishment springs. So important for grievers, the well represents our access to Source, that life-sustaining place of creativity that resides in each of us. This healing force quenches a thirst for our deep human need to understand life and death. We must realize that at some point, we have to surrender if we are to do more than just survive our grief. To surrender isn't to give up. It's to give *over*. Demeter's surrender at the well shows us that giving our grief *over* to some kind of inner strength and wellspring is necessary if our grief is to initiate a transformation. Loss, the story says, is like a piece of sand that eventually becomes a pearl. When a grain of sand slips into an oyster shell, then rubs against the soft mollusk within, it causes an irritation. The oyster coats the grain of sand with its own tissue until an iridescent gem is formed.

The gnawing pain of grief can hone us, like the pearl, into becoming more than we'd previously been.

As Demeter tends the hearth, we're also shown a symbol of fire, which represents our spirit, the *fire in the belly* of each of us. Fire is a metaphor for our connection to the essential stardust from which we humans are born. This symbolizes the necessity for turning toward our own unique values and beliefs as a source of spiritual rejuvenation and returning to who we truly are. During the year after my family died, I explored my spirituality, often through dreams in which Lois appeared—always bringing me a message of some kind. I found sustenance there, and inner peace amid my sorrow. My beliefs about the visible and invisible worlds took shape. As grievers, Demeter's fire-tending lays a soulful image at our feet. She's giving us a directive: examine your eternal Self and discover your true nature. She's showing us that it's time to start wondering about what makes you, unequivocally, *you*. Like Demeter, tending to your inner hearth is how you will engage this important inquiry, asking yourself to examine who you are and what holds spiritual meaning for you.

The Stepping Stones pathway is full of soulwork practices which provide opportunities for doing just that—discovering your Self. I capitalize the word "Self" to define a greater identity than that of your personality. There is more to who you are than a bundle of outer personas, job titles, body images, or personality traits. "Self" is distinguished from the noncapitalized word "self" in depth psychology. It's a way of describing the archetype of one's wholeness, one's true nature. The Persephone and Demeter myth says that when we are no longer who we once were, tending to and connecting with our spirituality is essential to the initiation of a new Self.

The myth hardly tells us anything about Persephone, who is now living in the Underworld, the Land of the Dead, where she undergoes the well-known tumult of puberty. We can't see the actual unmaking of the carefree child, but we know that she is dying to the innocent maiden she once was. We understand the necessity for her to go through the gauntlet of that hormonal passage in order to enter adulthood. But the myth offers more than that. It says that every loss is a death. While we may be grieving some*one* who died or some*thing* lost (as in the death of a job, marriage, or role), our own identities are undergoing death throes. Symbolic death is upon us, as Persephone's sojourn in the Underworld reveals. By the end of the story, just as she is released from the Underworld, Persephone willingly eats three pomegranate seeds, ensuring her return to the land of the dead for three months each year. This act suggests that a willingness to be unmade by our losses secures our initiation into a new form. When she emerges, Persephone is transformed, standing in her true, matured identity as Queen of the Underworld. Without reservation, she takes full ownership of the transformation she's undergone. You will, too, as you find courage to descend into the underworld of your grief.

The myth ends with the two goddesses standing arm in arm, celebrating their wholeness. Demeter has tossed off that old gray cloak and shines fully, resplendent in her mystical light. Persephone stands tall, a woman unto herself. As they rise together, reunited and renewed, owning their connection to an expanded sense of Self, they stand as sentinels for our own initiatory potential. This is not a sure thing; the myth shows us that we must grapple with the dark night of the soul that mourning offers. When we do that, we can go through the maze of our mourning and come out the other side, revitalized through our encounter with metaphorical death and the physical deaths of our beloveds.

ONCE UPON A TIME

For grievers, the path through loss is personal and archetypal. That is why mythic stories help us heal our personal suffering. For people grappling with loss, archetypal stories have the power to lift us out of the details of our unique pain and open the way to universal solutions and unseen healing potentials. You may recall stories from childhood or your young adult years—fairy-tales, fables, mysteries, movies, or books, such as the Harry Potter stories, *Lord of the Rings*, *ET*, *Star Wars*, or *Siddhartha*—that took you to another world. Their wild and mysterious tales carve new, imaginal pathways in the brain. Simple opening words, "Once upon a time" or "In a land far, far away," take us out of our everyday selves and plop us right down in an otherworldly, non-ordinary time, a healing territory.

An example of this comes from a Tree of Living and Dying ceremony I led in Ashland, Oregon. Megan was in the circle. Her son, Keita, died several years before. She was bereft for a long time, blaming herself, feeling remorse and regret, and railing against his physical absence. Megan was flooded by grief. Yet when I invited the group to tell a story about their loved ones, she was inspired to make up a fairy tale. Beginning with the words "Once upon a time," Megan spoke about a drowning girl who eventually learned to breathe underwater. When the girl saw others drowning in the waters, she started helping them to the surface. Megan shared with me later that when she spoke this fable out loud, the simple opening words took her into that otherworldly, healing terrain. By speaking in the third person, Megan's metaphors birthed a new perspective for her. She marveled at how the heavy rawness of her "old grief story" effortlessly lifted. This is the power of mythic stories: the personal story still exists, but the archetypal one offers new ways for maneuvering through the loss. Megan said, "This is powerful. I found a creative way of navigating my wrenching pain. Now I'm at the beginning of a whole new, healing phase."

When Lois died, I, too, called upon symbolic terrain as I wandered the desert of my lost identity. Like Persephone, I was abducted, hijacked by my grief. And like Demeter, I was cocooned in a tattered gray cloak. I understood that I wouldn't be returning to *normal* any time soon. I went back to work but soon gave notice that I was leaving. For a while, all I wanted to do was clean closets, then the garage. I was compelled. There was no rhyme or reason to it. But it soothed me. Put my outer world in order while my inner one was in disarray. This went on for months. I surrendered. I left my job and closed my private SoulWorks counseling practice. One day, tired after a thousand trips to Goodwill with boxes of *stuff*, I felt a tiny creative urge. I collaged a small box—a tiny casket—with images that connected me to Lois. I filled it with small items that symbolized roles that had previously animated me, including my SoulWorks business card and a collection of heart-shaped rocks on the doorstep to the cabin of the camp I lovingly directed. I put my name tag as executive director of a nonprofit in it, and a charm given by someone whose friendship I could no longer accept. On Post-It notes, I wrote old habits like overeating and overmanaging and put them in the box. These identities, and more, were no longer me; they filled that casket. My heart was heavy. I was saying goodbye to the me I'd been. She had filled me up in the past but no more. I put a heart stamp on the casket and addressed it: "To the Underworld." I wrote, then inserted, a letter to Persephone, Queen of the Underworld. I petitioned her for help through my dark time, saying, "I am on the precipice of death, the death of so many roles of my life. Endings are new beginnings . . . this I know. Yet for a new beginning to emerge, I need to accept these losses. Please help me!" I took the casket on a pilgrimage through the pristine mountains of the Sierra Madre. Together we gazed at wide vistas and tumbling waterfalls until finally we sat beside a wide creek. I imagined it as the River Styx, the wellspring of the mythological river that runs between heaven and earth. I took a deep breath, hugged that tiny coffin to my chest, and with all my love, tossed it into cold rushing waters in hopes it would, symbolically, reach Queen P. in the Underworld. Right then and there, as I watched it sink out of sight, I promised myself that Lois's death, and my grief, would not be without meaning.

Rituals are vessels for emotions. Channeling feelings through symbolic action speaks directly to our soul. This offers movement rather than the static recycling of our same tears. It allows our grief to reshape itself. Like mythic stories, rituals open creative brain pathways that initiate healing. My inventive ceremony was no exception. It enabled me to let go; it was my *surrender at the well* and the beginning of my journey toward greater wholeness. Symbolically enacting the myth was a conscious way to engage with the dismantling that was already underway in me. It gave me solace and the patience I needed. Rather than being at the mercy of inner disintegration, I chose it.

Making this choice is important for all of us. We must accept the demise of our old self, just as a caterpillar does when spinning a cocoon in which the old form dies. It is a necessary choice if we are to emerge from grief the way a butterfly emerges from a cocoon. Take heart in this archetypal story. While yours is personal, the mythic one offers itself as a source of comfort along your path. It's an affirmation that, by saying yes to your metaphorical inner deaths and finding acceptance for the literal ones, you will find a greater sense of Self and renewal through your loss and grief. When I carried out that ceremony at the river, I was a long way from finding my own fire in the belly. But choosing to say yes to dissolution of what was no longer true was an important step on the path to a new me. And that will be an important step for you, too.

Chapter Four

THE POWER OF TELLING THE TALE

There is power in stories. Sharing them out loud, in writing, or in pictures so they are witnessed and reflected back increases their power. Tracking our stories helps us untangle the knots in our hearts, trust our inner wisdom, and gather our unique strength. One woman in a Loss to Legacy program found this to be true. Raised to keep her emotions private, she slowly took the risk to share intimate stories of her forty-year love affair with Dale, her suddenly deceased husband. She told us about her trembling knees during her 1945 solitary pilgrimage at midnight, riding a city bus for the first time to welcome him home from the war. She described in detail the holy moment when her ruby red lips met his. How they went back to her little apartment, not yet married but ready to lie beside each other, sealing their love. As Emily allowed her heartache to be witnessed, she became more and more brave. She created a book that told their love story in photographs. Picture by picture and story by story, Emily's mourning eased, and her face took on the wistful eyes of a love-struck younger woman. Soon she found courage in other ways. Living alone became less daunting. Being open with her feelings came more easily. Stepping outside her comfort zone was possible. I ran into Emily recently. She said that the simple act of sharing her stories over those six weeks was tremendously healing. It helped her take a next step toward her new, albeit solo, life.

Stories heal. And they reveal, over and over, how the patterns of our lives remain essentially the same, even though the characters that populate them may change. Recognizing these repetitions brings new perspectives to old ideas, habits, and behaviors. I know now, from tracking my own stories and discovering repeated themes, that the life, death, rebirth cycle is not one that is traversed once and done. It is a spiral path of awakening. I liken it to a mountain climb, circling around and around to the top, looking out at familiar vistas on each round with a more expansive perspective. William Stafford says, in his poem "The Way It Is," that there's an invisible thread running throughout our lives that never changes. He says that while seeing it may be hard, when you hold on to it through tragedy and death, you will never get lost. He reminds us to stay connected with the thread and never let it go. The thread is symbolic of our truest Self, our soul. Finding and holding on to it connects us with our eternal wholeness, something that exists in each one of us. As I circled around the mountain of my losses, I held to that sometimes elusive, other times straightforward thread. I discovered that "my story" is really many stories, like many threads woven together, sometimes tangled and knotted and other times smooth as silk. Effortlessly, images and memories of my past with Lois and my family emerged. And tales of my Ancestors, people I knew and many I could only imagine, began taking on new meaning. At first, all the memories were of times when my parents, Lois, and Dave were ill. Images of the tumult and traumas of our lives filled me. I recalled tender caregiving, eliciting tears and evoking exhaustion. Sometimes, I just went numb. I was focused on their absence and their illnesses, not the entire life we shared before that. But ever so slowly, I remembered a bigger story of us, what I call the *long body* of the relationship, the complete picture of who and what we were to one another.

I began recalling the long body of my relationship with Lois with flashes of memory. Frozen treks through snow up to our knees. Layers of socks, gloves, scarves, and sweaters lying on radiators. Rubber boots drip-drying and laid out on newspapers on the speckled kitchen linoleum. Hot chocolate with tiny marshmallows melting in a mottled mustard-yellow, thick ceramic mug. Later, we had long-into-the-night conversations, out-of-state treks with boyfriends, and homemade pizzas piled high with vegetables. These memories fed me. Then, challenging memories came. Fights and misunderstandings. Distrust, betrayal, and hurt also surged between us like sharp rocks in our stream, building froth and fast water. I started remembering my parents' and grandparents' stories and their parents' tales, too. I shared them endlessly. I told funny ones and wept over sad ones. I joined a circle of soul seekers and spoke them in sacred council. I removed a door from a spare closet and turned it into an altar glowing with twinkling lights. I filled it with objects that told stories of my Ancestors and other people I'd loved while they were alive. It held the long body of my love.

The long body includes Ancestral patterns, ever-present in us even when we're unconscious of them or don't know who our Ancestors are. The power of our psyche to carry them is borne out in stories of children adopted as infants. I recall a tale of a Native American boy raised by a Jewish couple in New York City. When he turned thirteen and began preparations for his bar mitzvah, a Jewish coming-of-age ceremony, he began moving his body, flapping his arms in what his parents considered very strange movements. They took him to doctors and therapists to try to stop this unusual behavior. Eventually, an anthropological psychologist informed them he was dancing in patterns born of his lineage. He was enacting the rite-of-passage dance that all boys of his ethnic heritage performed at that age. The young man needed to enact his boy-to-man passage in a form coherent with his heritage, not just through his adoptive culture. The deep unconscious carries the power of the invisible thread that Stafford suggests in his poem. It's alive in our DNA.

Just months after Lois died, I picked up an Ancestral thread. I was on a retreat, taking a *dream walk* on the land. A dream walk is a process of consciously entering into symbolism and imagination in nature. I crossed a mossy log, a symbolic threshold between worlds, telling myself, *I am entering the dreamtime.* Unsure if anyone would show up, I invoked my Ancestors. Wandering on, I was palpably aware of my great-aunt Myrtle's presence, the energy between us vitally alive. I sat on a boulder overlooking a sunlit river, telling her how lost I felt without Lois, uncertain of who I was in the world. She reassured me, *You will know what to do when the time is right. You mustn't worry about money; we have your back.* With that, my whole lineage, known and unknown, passed through my body, back to front. I could feel my Ancestors touching my body, their substance thicker than smoke but less than water. In under two minutes, my concept of Ancestral lineage shifted on its axis. I grabbed hold of their now-tangible presence as the core of my spirituality. I fell into a connection I never before knew existed. Aunt Myrtle was showing me that Ancestors are real forces moving in our lives, the invisible thread Stafford wrote about in his poem. It was so powerful, I was weeping. I asked Aunt Myrtle if they were my tears or hers, and she said, *Oh no, my dear, they are all of our tears.* She was referring to the grief of our whole human collective. We all grieve. We all have sorrow. We all bemoan senseless violence, war, and loss of life. And we all mourn the tremendous degradation and deaths on our beautiful planet. She spoke, then, about my clan's love for the beauty of nature and the importance of caring for what we love. I saw myself as one link in a never-ending line of souls tethered to a thread of Ancestral potency. Trust blossomed. Lois or no Lois, I would never fully lose my way. That was abundantly clear with her next message: *There is a place calling to you, that needs you. Be patient. Don't try to figure it out yet. Just trust that you have a mission ahead. It involves the rainbow bridge.* I pondered. If people fall in love with the splendor of the earth, will they will care for her? Was that the mission before me? What in the heck did she mean by the rainbow bridge? But Aunt Myrtle said to be patient and not try to figure it out. So I waited.

This story and so many others are essential threads in my personal mythology. Each one a single strand among many, the warp and weft woven together as a whole new story of *me*. My great aunt's missive about patience, while challenging in this world of instant gratification, is important for us all. As we revisit the long body of our love and loss in right timing, our exploration of the past helps us write a new story. A new future, each tale a part of the whole incredible tapestry of you. This is the power of story.

TWO RARE BIRDS

Lois wanted to write *her* story into a book about how she and Dave awakened to love through cancer. I once called her a rare bird and her immediate response was, "That's the name of our book! *Two Rare Birds*!" When she died before recovering enough energy to do it, I added the tag-line *A Legacy of Love* and made it mine. Without knowing anything about writing a book or the power of storytelling, I began. It became a sacred path that led to my healing. I wrote about our sisterhood, our Ancestors, and the myriad life lessons Lois and Dave's cancer journey taught me. How they declared, over and over, that *cancer will not define us!* How, because the scalpel to her brain compromised Lois's language functions, she danced her eulogy to our dad instead of speaking it. How whispering in the darkness of one sleepless night about her soon-to-be-crafted memorial taught me the true meaning of legacy. How a mysterious beauty filled the room as Lois grew closer to death. In the book I inscribed her final surrender, her last breath, and the holy time afterward. That story bears recounting:

> Lois exerted her right to choose how she wanted to go, right up through these last days, as she gave herself over to love entirely. She'd reached a kind of surrender that is hard to fathom. Even on her deathbed, she exuded a kind of indescribable light. She was almost nonverbal, nearly completely paralyzed, and in tremendous pain, yet still radiant and glowing. Though it will sound like overkill, she was beatific. Being with her was compelling. What had mattered most became tangible, as love filled her room. Divine, beautiful Love.
>
> Lois's head was turned toward the window with eyes open but not seeing—at least not anything of this world. Her breathing intensified, with a quiet inhale and forceful exhale. Our unspoken intention was to bear witness to this holy act as she gathered steam to birth herself into the Great Beyond, whatever that may be. It seemed she was searching for the path out of her body, each pause between breaths a contraction through which Lois was birthing herself into another level of consciousness. Like in the final moments of childbirth, I thought to myself, "Push!" Lois's breath finally became quieter, more refined, then almost imperceptibly, it stopped altogether. She was, indeed, truly gone.
>
> We had been present to the mystery of life and death. We'd witnessed the birth of a soul moving out of life—from incarnation to dis-incarnation. We moved through the house in a surreal state of being, as if we, too, were standing at the gates of the Beyond. A veil had parted and we'd touched the ephemeral lands of spirit, and the sacredness of the passage we'd witnessed stayed with us. We agreed: dying is a lot like birthing.

Recounting each story filled my whole body, mind, and spirit. Little by little, one story led to another until, page after page, I wrote myself into a new understanding of who and what Lois and I had been to one another. The story of the lives and deaths of my whole family and my tumultuous relationship with Lois took form on the page. Since our sister-love was a roller coaster of laughing 'til we cried and turnabouts of jealousy and betrayal, I told all the stories. Including our conflicts was crucial. One day I was writing how Lois and I fought as kids and adults. Unexpected words flowed from my fingers onto the keyboard with a powerful insight: Lois and I weren't just fighting our own fights.

We were carrying out the habits of our father's father and his parents, trapped in a small shtetl—an eastern European village—in which persecution and conflict undermined safety and ease. The whole family would hide each Sunday, when church bells rang out indicating that gangs of Cossacks would soon be riding through the little streets, performing violence against Jews. They suffered until my great-grandmother, Bubba, who I knew only by reputation as a tough broad, escaped with her eight children, immigrating to Ellis Island. In this new land, frightened and uncertain, she motivated her children through competition. Conflicts between siblings became the norm, and distrust proliferated. My Pop-Pop did the same with his kids, until arguments became common. As we waged war against one another, Lois and I were fighting Ancestral battles from before we were born, perhaps in an attempt to right wrongs. My storytelling helped me discover that this conflict between family members was built into my Ancestors' patterns. Love and mistrust, hand-in-hand, all the way back through time. The potency of our DNA lived in Lois and me, carried out in our hurts, loves, wounds, and passions. It lives in all of us. We may not be able to escape our Ancestral inheritances, but I know we can break their chain and heal the patterns when we become conscious of them. Lois and I did that. We resolved rifts between us before she died. I am grateful beyond measure for the power of that forgiveness. I know that many people don't have that blessing. They are left with the challenge of sorting out conflicts with loved ones after they die. That's tough. Though many people think that unhealed relationships are forever doomed, that's not true. While it takes steadfast intention to settle those unfinished struggles and hurts, it's more than possible. I've witnessed the resolution that can come from letter writing, ceremonies, dreams, and many exercises offered in the Stepping Stones workbook.

In bringing conscious the patterns of interaction between Lois and me, I realized that while I am the outcome of all who have come before me, I am also my own person. With more awareness of what I was carrying on behalf of my father, grandfather, and great-grandmother, I would temper my DNA with forgiveness and the love I witnessed in Lois and Dave's story. If you don't know the people in your bloodlines, then your stories of adoption, foster families, or extended clans have equal power to shed light on who you are. Even without details of your lineage, your stories of wounds and traumas, when told with compassion, have the power to awaken your insights. I witnessed this in a Tree of Living and Dying ceremony in which we honored Ancestors through storytelling. One woman, whose life in foster care was troubled, shared how little she knew of her Ancestors. Though it was painfully different from mine and others, she still had a story to tell. She chose to honor the unknown people who gave her life by sharing it, telling me later that the act of publicly revealing her story brought healing. Storytelling, whatever the story contains, has power.

Lois's death plunged me into the underworld and storytelling was the path of my reemergence. By the time *Two Rare Birds: A Legacy of Love* was published, it wove a complete overhaul of me, or at least of who I'd known myself to be. I was changed through the story of life, illness, and death with Lois, and even more so by its telling. I started out lost, and by sharing my stories, I began feeling found. And you can find yourself, too.

Chapter Five

MINING FOR GOLD

The courage to say yes to all of your stories, and to death, can be scary, even if it holds the promise of growth. Digging up painful memories is counterintuitive; why mess with what has been tucked away or well buried? I think of it this way: When an untreated scrape goes unexamined, its likelihood of infection is high. Yet appropriate treatment leads to healing. This is equally true for the psyche; whole-person wellness comes with introspection and exploration. Imagine this examination as a pilgrimage—a risk-taking, soulful adventure into the mysterious territory of unexpected encounters and fortuitous synchronicities. These unforeseeable surprises can influence and re-form your identity.

We've all been hurt through myriad losses—some of us more dramatically than others, but no one escapes life without suffering. The specific set of losses and wounds we've been dealt are the very raw material from which our gifts are crafted. Finding treasures hidden within your grief asks you to dig in, to search, and to reflect on painful territory. Leonard Cohen speaks to the great beauty of this challenge in his song "Anthem." Whenever I hear the song's chorus about there being a crack in everything and how that crack is how the light gets in, I am moved by this truth. Reflecting on the cracks that loss has wreaked on your heart is the way to let in your light and begin to shine it brightly, first for yourself and, ultimately, for others. I've seen this principle of finding light through the cracks with clients and in the world around me. I've seen stories of neglect inspire a commitment to be more responsive to others. I've observed how feeling demeaned can invite an attitude of inclusivity toward all people. For some, abuse clarifies the importance of kindness. Habits of fear can give way to courage. One student translated the death of a baby brother into a career as a hospice nurse. Another, her father's illness into a career in cancer-care. Emotional wounds are a part of the human condition. How we choose to relate to them determines our ability to grow. When we rail against the injustices of our wounding there is power in that. But that resistance can also cause stasis, with the potential of turning against us. Victims become perpetrators, unresolved wounds repeating from one generation to the next. Making a choice to think of pain and loss as an opportunity, therby revisiting what is important and has meaning, enables us to move beyond our wounds to discover their gifts.

Saying yes to a mining expedition into grief is a far cry from doing the actual excavation. Drilling down in order to unearth a new layer of authenticity takes courage. Yet mining the strata of loss chisels away at old habits. It breaks open familiar routines until old forms of engaging with oneself and the world fall away. At least that's what happened for me. Lois's terminal diagnosis led to a profound moment of coming to terms with my own mortality. The realization that life is truly fleeting inspired previously harbored resentments to fall away between us. Yet that only heightened my remorse for the time we lost to our rivalry and strife. We could have relished our comforting sisterhood instead. I broached this topic while she lay dying. "Lo, I wish we'd healed our rifts sooner." While she didn't have many words left, she turned her big brown, loving eyes to me and replied, "You can't wish for what you can't have." That said it all. What was done could not be undone. Sad as that was, it left me wondering, ever more deeply, at my own culpability in the betrayals between us. After she died, I mulled this over again and again. Eventually I discovered, much to my ego-shattering dismay, that I inherited a personality trait from my father's clan. Perfectionism, making righteous justifications and judgmental assessments of others, had become an ingrained habit. I was humbled to understand that this way of relating permeated my life. I vowed to make a change. That's easier said than done. I still have to work hard at my habitual responses to life. But I knew this realization was the crack that would let far more light into my life. And it did. And has. With a diligence toward practicing forgiveness, first toward myself, then toward others, I could turn that humiliating pattern around. I practiced bringing more grace into my interactions. While that has changed the nature of some relationships, others have fallen away. That's painful. But ultimately, it's been freeing. Reflecting on the cracks in your losses, the deep crevices of remorse, regret, anger, or unresolved issues, is arduous. There's no way around that. You can only go *through* it. Yet not doing that hollowing out is equally painful. It can be potentially heart-hardening. Or numbing. It can cut you off from life-changing growth. It can circumvent your healing. I found my way through it, and I know you can too.

Seeking an inner voice of wisdom is key to finding the courage to undertake that track. It's not the only way to create new habits and grow from your losses instead of being stuck in them. But looking within is sustainable and stabilizing. Finding my wisdom required unearthing all I'd learned from living alongside Lois and Dave through their cancer journey. They fought hard to live, but when the time for dying approached, they found acceptance, and there was simplicity and beauty in that. I learned that beauty can be found anywhere, even in the saddest moments. Their gratitude for kindness from neighbors, coworkers, and friends was so encompassing that I often came home from a visit of caregiving as if I'd been on retreat rather than in the throes of a cancer-filled household. I've adopted their accepting stance as an approach to my own death whenever it may come. Knowing unequivocally that I will die and that many other people I love will also die gives me a profound gratitude for life. In spite of the turmoil of the world and the everyday losses that screech out over the news (or the ones I encounter in my aging body), I focus on this gratitude as a legacy born of Lois and Dave's lives and deaths. And that brings gentleness to the fore. Purple tulips in bloom, the scent of fresh air on the wind, or a dog warming my feet is an opportunity for pleasure. Tiny moments like these add up to more than the sum of their parts. They replace thinning reserves of emotional strength. They add inner resilience. They build capacity for enduring sorrow. I imagine the spirits of my Ancestors flourishing when I appreciate what they gave me. I hear them in my mind's ear reminding me to lighten up when I'm caught in everyday angst. I wonder what your loved ones would wish for you to carry forth as the legacy from their lives and deaths. Whatever that is, it's unlikely that they would want you to cut off from life entirely. You can find space for sorrow *and* the ability to shine in remembrance of their lives. These seeming opposites can live side by side. It's your choice. Because you get to decide when, where, and how deep, you dig.

I shoveled through layers of lessons that my family's illnesses taught me. With the tenacity of a miner searching for riches, I considered how my father grappled with Parkinson's and kept a positive demeanor despite the vitality it stole from him. As his immense fortitude morphed into surrender and gentle vulnerability, I witnessed a softening of his previously razor-sharp edges. I choose, not always, but when I can, to adopt his sweetness and positivity in place of my prior perfectionism. When Alzheimer's transformed my mother into an unrecognizable personality, I wondered about the difference between the true essence of a human being's spirit and their persona. In spite of her diminishing self, I saw my mother as the graceful figure she'd been throughout my life. I focused on that, realizing that nothing could take it away. I chose to honor the kindness of her essential character by being more tender and accepting. This changed my tolerance for my own fallible humanity. I thought about the privilege it was to care for all of them during their final days. Keeping my dad's mouth moist. Cleaning the bedpan. Administering medications. Holding Dave as he wept when Lois took her last breath. As all these sad memories became sacred moments of a deeper love than I'd known before, my own identity grew exponentially. As I treasured, above all else, the bigger-than-life gift of love that Lois gave me in her dying, forgiveness became my motto and trust became my modus operandi. These gifts were a warm blanket woven from my initiation by death and grief. It gently covered my sorrow.

Your lessons will surely be different from mine. They are your own, born from a completely different set of circumstances. I believe that your story, if you search deeply, has a gift for you regardless of the suffering it contains. I don't know where or how it will unfold. Only you know that. I do trust this: in the center of it all lies your heart's wisdom. Seek that well at the center of your soul, uncomfortable feelings and all. Whatever you feel—hurt, anger, remorse, or unbearable sorrow—I am confident that is where you will find everything you need.

Lonnie came to one of my programs called Intimate Conversations. We were sharing stories and breaking taboos by discussing death. He was angry about his partner's death, how Sandi died completely cut off from her feelings, addicted to numbing out with television. There was no consciousness in her dying, no heartfelt goodbye to Lonnie or her kids. Nothing to soothe Lonnie's grief. As he dug into his rage, Lonnie discovered he had a habit of emotional repression from a disconnected family system. While Sandi became more and more depressed by her illness, Lonnie, too, retreated, cut off from his own sadness. He stoically cared for Sandi in her final days, disconnected from love. As he recounted the trauma, Lonnie recognized that he mirrored her pattern. Sandi wasn't the only one cut off from feeling. As Lonnie began talking more openly about his feelings, he created new, more emotionally satisfying relationships with others. As he began practicing new behaviors, Lonnie slowly broke the chain of isolation born of that hardened habit.

Another client, a Loss to Legacy group participant, learned about herself from the deep regret she felt about her husband's failed cancer treatments. She lamented the lost quality of life in his last months. Railing against a medical system that pushed quantity of life over quality was painful. The finger-pointing and blaming was easier than digging into her own psyche, but it only increased her suffering. Joanie began exploring her remorse more deeply, determined to break this pattern. She realized she had a habitual tendency to give away her power to outer authority. With deeper mining into that habit, Joanie understood that she needed to listen more carefully to the quiet voice of her inner wisdom. She turned toward that capacity and started making new choices about where and how she would live. When she moved to her new home, the pain of her grief lightened. She began to talk about the beauty in her pain. She embraced the opportunity to grow through her sorrows and turned her attention toward bringing more lessons from her loss into her life ahead.

I heartily believe that by digging below your surface, like me, Lonnie, and Joanie, you will find treasures. Once they have been excavated, you will be able to carry them as gifts that honor your loss and soften your sorrow.

Chapter Six

MORE THAN A NEW NORMAL

"New normal" is the phrase Lois and Dave used as cancer exacted one loss after another. It describes accepting the losses and changes that come with illness as the new normalcy of daily living. "More than a new normal" takes that a step further. It refers to growth that goes beyond acceptance of loss, to transforming it into something more. There were certainly times when the most Lois and Dave could do was cope, and sometimes just barely. Surely, you have felt that way in your early stages of grief. Yet their goal was never to stay in that state of "just managing" for long. Lois asked, time and again, "What am I supposed to *learn* from this double-cancer story?" Dave said, "It's more than a double-cancer story; it's a double-love story. Because look at all the love we've received and awakened to *through* it." They found a way for their spirits to thrive, even as their bodies were barely surviving. That's what made them rare birds and how their new normal grew larger than their old way of living in the world. I was inspired to do the same.

We talked about this in a Legacy Story Circle. Barry shared about his brother, who died young from a biking accident. Only twenty-three at the time, Barry was depressed for years, until he realized that life's length and breadth are a mystery. As he faced and then accepted that truth, Barry began looking at his brother's death as a wake-up call. He said, "You never know . . . *I'll* never know how much time I have left." Once he had the sense that life ". . . can end anytime. It's so capricious, so unknown," he told himself, "Don't wait, Barry!!" He went on to say that just "doing something different" became really important to him—that the realization of life's frailty pushed him past his comfortable boundaries. Barry changed his career, moved across the country, married impulsively, and started growing. He said that "... it's changed how I live *now* ... all these twenty years later ... with more courage, and stamina, and dedication to my own life." He finished by defining something essential that had been lingering at the edge of his awareness for years. Reflectively, with unfolding clarity, he shared, "The other side of post-traumatic stress is post-traumatic growth. That's my brother's legacy to me." Barry's story reminded me of my own.

My more than a new normal came into focus a year after my mother's death and ten months after Lois's. Sally and I met at Lois and Dave's house in Austin, Texas, for Dave's memorial. The day after celebrating Dave's life amid fields of bluebonnets, Sally and I, with Mom's ashes in hand, wandered to the wide Pedernales River in search of a waterfall. We knew that our mother, a self-proclaimed "waterfall freak," would delight in our goodbye ceremony in one of her favorite places. After navigating piles of white limestone rocks to and from a secluded spot, we returned to the comfort of Lois and Dave's forest-green couch. Empty and emotionally drained, we sat silently in the waning light of sunset. The half-dismantled house filled our hearts and the space between us with sorrow. Suddenly, Sally took a big breath and burst out, "We could start a foundation in their honor!" We brewed on the idea for months. What would we call it? What would it do? In the pit of my stomach I knew that, though it was Sally's brainstorm, it was mine to carry out. Sally often said that *Two Rare Birds* needed to be written first. She knew it would guide us to our mission.

A vision began to form. I began thinking of death as a spiritual matter. When the body dies, what happens to the soul? When the physical reality is no more, what is our spiritual reality? And why is talking about death so taboo in our culture? These questions populated my mind constantly. One day while driving mindlessly, Aunt Myrtle's cryptic words about my mission of serving the rainbow bridge came to mind. Was the rainbow bridge an underlying principle of our nonprofit foundation? Curious, I researched and learned that the rainbow is a worldwide, cross-cultural, archetypal symbol for a bridge between worlds, and the connection between spirit and matter. Was the rainbow bridge an answer to my contemplations? As Sally and I reflected on this, we recounted a story, an uncanny moment we had shared: I walked down a gritty Oakland street, talking with her on the phone on my way to work. We told each other that, though the doctors weren't saying so, we knew Lois was close to death. I spied a tarot card lying upside down in the gutter, pockmarked from recent rains. I interrupted Sally midsentence: "Whoa! There's a tarot card in the gutter!" Since Sally's immediate response was, "Well, pick it up!" I scooped up the weather-beaten card and turned it over. It was the Sun card, a mountaintop enfolded by a circular rainbow linking the twelve zodiac symbols. *It must represent wholeness*, we thought. Sally looked it up online and we learned that it was about the reconstruction that comes from destruction. Rebirth following death. It was a synchronistic sign from the universe, affirming our intuition about Lois's pending death and our eventual resurrection from grief. Lois's medical professionals declared her "terminal" within days.

As we talked about our idea of a nonprofit foundation the memory of that synchronicity became another sign. We thought of the tiny Hebrew letter, *resh*, at the bottom of the Sun card. In the mystical teachings of the Kabbalah, resh refers to the place of divine illumination, a connection point between spirit and matter. This is what our nonprofit would be about! Talking about this connection would lift conversations about death to a new level. As the project moved from infancy to incorporation, the time for naming arrived. We wanted a word that symbolized a connection with the wholeness of life and death, including the soulful connection between the two. When we simultaneously realized that resh is a rainbow bridge, without hesitation, we named our nonprofit Spirit of Resh Foundation. Our logo, an image of a rainbow connecting earth with sky, shows the important connection between humans and their beloved dead. Aunt Myrtle was right. Serving the rainbow bridge *is* my mission. Once these ideas took hold, I started envisioning my new life and it unfolded. I kept saying yes. Just as Resh received the federal government's sanctification as a fully fledged 501.c3 nonprofit corporation, our first grant award came through. We received funds for publishing *Two Rare Birds: A Legacy of Love*. The funding covered a small book tour. Little did I suspect how my trip to share the book at a Portland conference would carry me further into my *new normal*. I was on my way back home to California when I stopped in the quaint village of Ashland, Oregon. The town was awash with color and scent, a rainbow of flowers. Out of the blue, I heard the phrase *this place smells like home*, inside my head. Thirty years ago, I'd said those very words to Lois as we disembarked from a train in Oakland. It was there that I met Seth, the love of my life, married, and expressed my passion in purposeful work.

That salt-scented Oakland air reminded me of my childhood home near the Chesapeake Bay, but the landlocked, decidedly *not* salty-aired Ashland was far from smelling even faintly of home. Seth and I had been longing for more beauty and serenity of nature in our everyday living and were contemplating a life away from the big and crowded city of Oakland. With the synchronicity of hearing that unbidden phrase, I knew instantly that southern Oregon was meant to be our new home. I called Seth and said, "It's Ashland! We're moving to Ashland!" His beautiful response: "Okay." I felt as if Lois had whispered that phrase into my mind. I sent up a brief prayer of gratitude: *Thanks, Lo!*

A few months later we returned, went for a drive, and fell in love with Applegate Valley—an hour outside Ashland. Remembering Aunt Myrtle telling me *There is a place in the world that is calling to you*, Seth and I said *Yes!* in a now-or-never, you-only-get-one-life kind of way. Four years after that infamous year of death, my husband, Seth, our golden retriever, Shayna, and I moved lock, stock, and barrel from creative but concrete-jungled Oakland to Applegate Valley. We landed on twenty awe-inspiring acres of quiet. When we lost count of the rainbows we saw from our lodge-like windows, Seth named our setting the Sanctuary at Rainbow Ridge. I created a hermitage on our property to host one-person-at-a-time soul retreats. I tend both the Foundation and the Sanctuary with loving devotion. I grow food and flowers, offer community storytelling ceremonies, and support people who are ready to transform their losses into legacies. I am living a life I could barely have imagined while Lois was alive. I feel her presence in everything I do. All that I have received from her is part of me now. This life in Applegate Valley, Oregon, is Lois's legacy to me.

As Aunt Myrtle recommended, finding this *more than a new normal* required a lot of patience. All those years back, as I lamented my loss of self, I had no inkling that this would be how I found my way back into life. Finding this place where Spirit of Resh Foundation makes its home and where people fall in love with the beauty of nature is more than worth the wait. I pass Aunt Myrtle's wisdom to you: hold faith that one day you will find a more-than-just-coping-with-your-grief life. Your new form is waiting for you, calling to you, ready for you. You will come to it in time. As in gardening, the process takes patience and tending, not pushing and demanding. The seeds of your eventual transformation can be planted once you clear away debris. Watering those seeds with your tears helps them germinate. Slow fertilization from the compost of your inner work will feed those tiny new shoots. And your ongoing surrender to the ebb and flow of the light and dark, sorrow and joy, enables your strong new Self to grow, then thrive.

This is true for all of us. I continue shedding and pruning away what no longer serves as I practice new attitudes and actions. I envision my life in fresh, new ways, knowing that it is a continual work in progress, as am I. Learning not to tug impatiently on my sprouting Self still isn't easy, but I practice trust even when I'm not feeling it. Coming into a renovated sense of purpose, a reason to get up in the morning, meant that I had to get out of my own way. I couldn't figure any of it out in advance. And neither can you. I simply needed to become willing to dive deep into the midst of my pain in order to grow and find renewed meaning. I propose that you can, and will, too.

Chapter Seven
LIVING LEGACY

We are each given a legacy. We live that legacy and then leave one when it's our turn to depart from this life. Though many of us may not like the life we were born into, it's up to us to learn and grow from what we inherited in order to create our most authentic life, our living legacy. A legacy is what you leave in your own wake, a physical or virtual expression of the sparkling gems developed from sharing your story, mining your gold, and finding a vision for a *more-than-new-normal* life. In a deeper sense, it is an ever-evolving work in progress, an everyday way of living and belonging to the world. That is a living legacy.

Judy, a Loss to Legacy participant, began expressing her living legacy when she accepted responsibility for creating a footstone and unveiling ceremony at her mom's grave. In Jewish tradition, this is supposed to happen on the first anniversary of the death, but Judy was too bereft and grief-disorganized to do it. As the second anniversary approached, she knew it was time to start the process. Her mother wasn't a traditionalist but was a woman of integrity who kept her word, known among beloveds as the one everyone could rely on. Judy, determined to step up to the task, found herself stumped when it came to engraving words on Rosalie's footstone. The process of naming the legacy of one human being, in just a few words, can be daunting. What *are* the right words? How can a whole life be gathered onto a gravestone? What is the essence by which this person's life will be memorialized forever? Judy, like all of us, longed for inspiration and to get it just right. She wanted the stone to reveal Rosalie's essential character, her passion for the arts, devotion to friends and family, and generosity to many humanitarian causes. Judy dug deep into this soul-worthy and creative challenge. She emerged from her underworld reflection with a meaningful phrase that reflected her mother beautifully: "She made her life a work of art through caring deeds and a loving heart." Having grown from innocence to competence, empowered with self-trust, and nourished by this act, Judy created and led the graveside ritual with reverence, presence, and remembrance, honoring her connection with family and her Ancestral lineage. Through all this Judy realized how much it matters to follow in her mother's footsteps and to be known as a woman of her word: creative, reliable, and trustworthy. As she carries her mother's caring spirit of service into her community of family and friends, Judy is crafting her own living legacy every day.

Living legacies unfold into the world, becoming inspiration for everyone. They have a life of their own, expanding beyond our personal need to heal. That was true for Judy, and its true for me through Resh. Resh's mission of using story to inspire building a relationship with death that informs our lives is tied to a set of principles drawn from Lois and Dave's lives and deaths. I try to live by them every day as best I can. Here are those principles:

Love is the connective tissue between all life. This principle was born of Lois's revelatory truth, powerfully experienced only once, under anesthesia, during her first brain surgery. She experienced the fabric of the universe as being made of love. She said, afterward, that love is all that matters. Shared countless times, like ripples moving outward in a pond, it speaks to the invisible, weightless web that connects us all. If this principle were one we all practiced, how different would our world be?

Life is precious; this moment is all we have. Lois often reminded me of life's impermanence and that this moment is all we have. When we discipline our minds to attend to this truth, we become more present to each moment of our lives, even the small, simple ones, not just the big, memorable ones. This enhances and changes the quality of every experience. I strive, mostly imperfectly, but with intention to improve, to live in a way that honors the passing moments of the life I've been granted. We never know when our final moment will come. I wonder what the world would be like if we all lived as though this day were our last.

Respect for all life builds vital, healthy communities. Lois and Dave's community was eclectic, filled with people from all walks of life. Lois, an environmental educator, understood the premise of diversity being essential to healthy ecosystems. On the eighty acres of public lands next to our twenty, I consider different life forms living in harmony, creating a healthy community. Dead trees build mounds of humus feeding new shoots. Edible mushrooms spring from under piles of leaves. Piles of bear scat disintegrate and the seeds within them become sprouts of baby manzanita trees fertilized by nitrogen in the poo. Wisdom received from all of this: everything has its purpose even when I don't understand it. Just as acceptance of death helps us appreciate being alive, respect for all forms of life awakens us to the necessity for appreciating differences. What if this respect were the driving force in our world?

The purpose of human life is to love, learn, grow, and serve. Lois and Dave learned about love through cancer. They grew in their capacity to find joy amid turmoil and troubles. Life is like a classroom where we are given lesson upon lesson. When we learn what those lessons were meant to teach, we grow. The lessons come in all forms, not the least of which is loss, perhaps the hardest of all. Learning and growing from loss gives it meaning. Meaning is the raw material for purpose. With purpose comes the ability to serve and the responsibility to pay it forward. When service comes from the heart, it's an antidote to suffering. Giving becomes a way of receiving. A world filled with service-driven legacies would be something, wouldn't it?

Honesty, expressed with compassion, builds intimacy and trust. This is as challenging as it is important. Lois and I struggled with our closeness, but it was only when we expressed hurt, hand-in-hand with compassion, that we found our way back to each other, rebuilding trust and intimacy. To have compassion literally means to suffer-with. Sitting in another person's seat and looking through their eyes with opened, listening hearts, we suffer-with one another's stories. This allows us to grow far beyond our wounds and betrayals. Being empathic with your story and others' builds trust and connection. A world that goes beyond political correctness and politeness into compassionate and authentic caring is one where all people experience safety. This is revolutionary!

Forgiveness is a path to healing. You have already read my story about healing rifts with Lois and the beauty of forgiveness between us. I've yet to meet someone who has lived a life without remorse for hurting others. Forgiveness for self and other, infused with accountability for one's actions, is a powerful release. Once forgiveness has taken hold, letting go of grudges and blaming, healing begins. True accountability takes our healing further. It requires us to learn from our remorse, forgive ourselves, and then change our behavior. This is beautifully humbling. What a world this would be if more people walked through each day without carrying resentment like baggage we can't put down.

It is up to each of us to make the most of the circumstances we are given by life. When she couldn't talk, Lois danced. She made the most of what she had, in spite of what she lost. Denying our circumstances doesn't make them go away; it just keeps us stuck and mired in the mud of victimhood, railing at what we are unable to change. Acceptance furrows the ground, turning our circumstances into rich soil that offers a foundation for growth. Then we can make the most with what we have. Dancing with what remains turns our eyes toward learning. This is empowering. It breaks us out of suffering over our pain. This is a worthy transformation, turning sorrow into a living legacy.

Trusting in the connection between that which is seen and unseen transforms fear into love. I carry the image in my mind's eye of a Star of David—a symbol of my Ancestral heritage. With two entwined triangles, one pointing up and the other, down, I understand it as a visual symbol of the seen and unseen as expressed by the Hermetic phrase "As above, so below." When I began thinking of Lois (as spirit) in the *above*, and me (as matter) in the *below*, with gossamer threads of a rainbow bridge between us, I started trusting that we are still entwined forever. This kind of trust brings us full circle, back to the first principle: *love*. Trusting in our Ancestors' presence in our lives has the power to transform our fears and sorrows into abiding love.

These principles are the foundation of my living legacy. Together they form my Legacy Mission Statements. I propose that we all have the capacity to create a set of principles that emerge from our losses. Yours will be your own. It's not necessary to move to another state, write a book, or start a nonprofit to take actions that form a new living legacy. It's much simpler than that. You can do it from right where you are.

Jeanie, a woman who attended one of the grief support groups I led, does this in a simple way. Her husband, Bob, who died from cancer, was a lover of beach and forest. He was a runner; she was not. After he died, she began jogging; it was a way Jeanie dealt with her grief. It connected her to Bob.

Eventually she started running 10-Ks, then half-marathons, and now, especially when they are held in adored forests, ocean-side, or along a lakefront, Jeanie runs full marathons. She's as surprised as anyone to find that she loves it. When Jeanie runs, tears often accompany the sweat rolling down her brow. But she says that they're tears of gratitude as much as they are of sorrow, because running is one way that Jeanie carries out Bob's legacy—so that their kids might know him through her.

Another woman, Laurel, joined a Legacy Story Circle and shared a simple practice that expresses her living legacy. At 55 years old, she's the last one standing in her family of origin. She doesn't have children but she has a niece who doesn't know her own father. Laurel said, "She happens to be really a big heart, amazing, bright—she's my bees-knees—the coolest thing." Since Laurel intimately knows the painful experience of fatherless-ness, because her own father died when she was twelve, Laurel feels a sacred responsibility for carrying forward a sense of the generations that came before with her beloved niece. When we talked about the idea of legacy, Laurel said that the way she lives, every day and in every way, is how she expresses legacy. In this gentle simplicity Laurel passes the torch of connection through love and presence with the people who matter to her.

Choosing how you carry out the values of your old life and live in accord with your lessons learned, the blessings among the curses, and new visions born from encountering death is what moves you forward. Your choices, how you relate with life from now on, ripple outward. It's like the butterfly effect, in which one simple movement, like the flapping of a butterfly's wing, can give rise to a tornado across a continent. This is a great metaphor for the way that a small change can create a big transformation. One small action here turns into an impact there. Each time someone finds meaning and purpose from their grief, then implements legacy-building actions, I am humbled by their courage. When I witness people tossing away old attitudes and adopting new ones, my faith in the resilience of the human heart is enhanced. Even though I know that grief will visit another day for all of us, I appreciate the tenacity, audacity, and dedication that take us through our gauntlet. We walk this path for ourselves and for one another. Each time someone chooses this Stepping Stone path to healing and transformation it strengthens my living legacy. And by sharing it with you, I strengthen yours. We are not alone; there are many walking beside us. Together, we stand at the threshold of this mighty path.

Section Two

AT THE THRESHOLD

Chapter Eight
SAYING YES

The death of someone we love is a road we'd rather not take. But finding ourselves no longer sure of who we are, like Dorothy in *The Wizard of Oz* trying to find her way home, we are cast into the journey. Sometimes we trek while kicking and screaming. Other times we navigate with ease, an inner GPS system guiding our way. Either way, we face the possibility of discovering new territory. Terrains where grace balances grief, new vistas are balm to our scathed and shattered selves, and furrowed soil is the ground for a restored spirit of living. After a beloved dies, when we don't know where the floor beneath our feet is, can't remember half of the conversations we had yesterday, and things that once had meaning are lost, new questions need to be asked. What matters most *today*? How do I maneuver this path that's been thrust on me? Where will I find meaning again, or purpose in living? Who am I, *really*? There may not be immediate answers, but to ask is worthy work—it ennobles our hearts. Without posing our questions, answers rarely come. Letting them remain unanswered for a time, with a willingness to listen patiently, opens the door for resolutions to arrive in their own time.

We have lost something precious, but we are still alive, in flesh and bone. That means we are given the possibility of learning and growing. Granted, no one treasures the tumultuous emotions that often accompany saying yes to death. But if death has entered your house, what is the alternative? The shadows of grief have already darkened your doorstep. So, what now? Say yes. Embrace it. Embrace all your losses. To accept them, your lost person, job, relationship, identity, and every nuanced absent part of your life is to invite your unknown Self to arrive. None of us can cure the past, but we can heal ourselves into the future. Accepting this enables us to rebuild.

You are at the threshold of an underworld journey that leads to healing. This metamorphosis comes with your commitment. A transformational journey is possible by following the steps laid before you. You will learn new practices or bring tucked-away skills out of the closet, dust them off, and use them liberally. It's not a straightforward route. Taking one small step at a time requires willingness. As you keep placing one foot in front of the other, you move forward. That movement is what matters most. It doesn't matter how fast or slow you go. Just keep moving. Take a first step. Say *Yes!*

LEGACY STORY: ABABIO'S YES

My friend and colleague Marilyn Ababio said yes. I met her when Spirit of Resh was barely born and I was still writing *Two Rare Birds*. In the way of outreach and networking, with one person leading me to another, I was introduced to her with a synchronistic timing that gave us both a big Yes! She was the director of a new, innovative project with the County of Alameda, in California, called Getting the Most Out of Life. It's grown now, far beyond its beginnings. Back then, it was simply dedicated to helping people accept the value of hospice long before reaching the final days of dying. At that time, the average hospice stay was less than two weeks; people thought it was just where they went to die. But hospice services are available for six months before that, and they include a wide array of services to both patients and their families. From social workers, to chaplains, nurses and medical directors, Hospice helps people live fully within their terminal diagnoses, offering quality of life, however much quantity remains, for those who can accept their inevitable final breath.

Ababio's (as I affectionately call her) twenty-year-old son, Musheer, died from leukemia. Like many people I've encountered, she was angry at the medical system, feeling that they failed to communicate the whole truth about Musheer's condition. They didn't prepare her for the eventuality of a second treatment failing. Instead, they simply forged on. Many people have told me they wish their loved ones had stopped treatments sooner, enabling a higher quality of life before their death. She said to me, "They tell you, but in such a way that they let the hope overwhelm the reality. Because that next treatment was a bad decision. They should have sat us down and made it clearer that, in spite of the hope, it was a futile idea. Then, I think we could've gotten ready for what was coming, sooner and better."

In Western culture, doctors are trained to preserve life at all costs—not to accept death. In the name of medicine, Musheer (like both Lois and Dave) continued with long, expensive treatments and surgeries that prolonged the quantity of his life, but not its quality. Ababio and I lamented this fact to each other time and again. That's why we were passionate about providing a different perspective to the world. It's what Getting the Most Out of Life was all about, helping others come to this realization for themselves, before it was too late.

Ababio generously shared her story with me. She began by saying that when Musheer died, she felt like the universe squeezed her so hard that she was just a pinhole of light. She told me, "I went to my knees because going to the ground was the only way I could feel anything." When her brother simply placed his hand on her back, Ababio could finally sit upright. That's when she began to bear her grief, finding strength by honoring who Musheer was while he'd been alive. Ababio recounted how he started changing her life at the memorial service as each of the men in her family got up to speak. One-by-one, in one form or another, they all said that Musheer made them want to be a better man. The way that he embraced life in the face of his illness set an example for the whole family. She told me about the night she and Musheer took a walk out onto a dock and he spoke words of wisdom beyond his years. She said, "He told me on the dock, 'Mom, maybe it's my destiny to die.' Somehow, he came to grips with the reality of his impending death, and he made something good out of it. He helped me see what I now believe: that when people feel like they have a destiny, when they feel they have a purpose, somehow their life is purpose-*full*." Musheer's surrender to the certainty of his death awakened Ababio to her own purposeful destiny, deeply connected to Musheer's life and his death. That was the beginning of Ababio's Yes.

Soon after Musheer died, Ababio's mom became ill. She said that when her mother needed a dose of truth-telling, Ababio gave it to her directly and with compassion. She told me, "My mom just came conscious one day and said, 'What am I doing here?' I said, 'You're dying, Mom'. And that truth gave her spiritual comfort. I decided I'm not going to be afraid of this end-of-life business. It's like, the reason I was born is to be able to give that kind of response."

Honesty, when expressed with compassion, deepens trust and intimacy. Ababio and her mom experienced a deep bond with that bold and loving statement of truth. How refreshing would it be if the medical system built compassionate truth-telling into its system? How much suffering would be avoided, not to mention costs?! Ababio went on to talk about her own truth-telling. "People need help getting through trying times. They need to be informed about what's happening around them. They need to be supported emotionally and spiritually, so that they can survive it. Because, when people lose their grounding, their footing, they need a way to stand in that fire. They need to feel that gentle pressure of a hand on their back offering support. I wanted to find a way to share my truth so that people understand that their pain is bearable. I wanted to be a force for reassuring them that the reason they are still alive, even if the most awful thing has happened to them, is because they're supposed to still be alive. I want people to know that they need to ask themselves, what is the meaning of my life and how do I give my life meaning?"

She did that. She built a living legacy that gave her life meaning after Musheer died. With passion for helping others be unafraid of death, she pulled me and others into her sphere. About her work she says, "I feel like I'm doing legacy-building work. We get to touch the souls of people. We get to touch people's hearts and have conversations that a lot of people don't dare have. And we get to encourage people. It's a story of love and community, and unity. And it's a positive thing, helping keep people who died alive in memory and spirit. That's legacy."

Marilyn Ababio was well on her way to changing the culture around end-of-life care in Alameda County's public health system, institutionalizing something that wasn't there before. She did all this and much more, with one small Yes when she was down on her knees. Then with another one at Musheer's memorial. Telling the truth to her mom when she told her that she was dying, Ababio said another Yes. One Yes built upon another, until they led to Ababio's living legacy, Musheer's destiny linked forever to hers.

While Ababio is now retired from Alameda County, her living
legacy continues at Comfort Homesake, the nonprofit she founded.
You can learn more about Ababio's "Yes" on their website: www.comforthomesake.com.

Chapter Nine
WRITING YOUR WAY HOME

Once you say yes, the real work begins. Writing, especially the stream-of-consciousness process of journaling, is one way to begin. It's a powerful method for coming home to yourself. Journaling is a long-standing process of personal inquiry, therapeutic self-exploration, and creative expression. A way to sift through and draw out emotions in order to deepen understanding of events. Writing things out is a release. It activates a different part of our brain than thinking or talking. Journaling allows us to take the lid off our feelings, let the steam out, and spill our ever-changing storm of emotions onto the private page. Anything is welcome there. It's where we step into the holy sanctum of our own voice. The blank page holds space for anything and everything: rage, hurt, relief, joy, longing, and despair are all welcome there. It's the temple where we can ride the waves of sorrow, anger, acceptance, trauma, or yearning until the waters recede and we find ourselves on the shores of our own inner wisdom. While some people say that writing by hand is a more felt or embodied experience, others prefer the ease of writing on a computer to elicit their memories and stories. Either way, people report feeling better after pouring their stories out onto a page. However we choose to do it, journaling is healing.

Your journal is where you may slowly unravel the tangled knot of your lived experience, loosening the strands until the threads can be rewoven into the finest tapestry of you. Bringing into the light what may have been pushed to the side, shoved under the carpet or lies at the bottom of your awareness may be a challenge. But when those unwelcome thoughts or feelings remain in the dark, they fester, much like mildew in a dank basement. Some grievers prefer to put it all away, put on a happy face, and try to get back to whatever normal can be mustered. But what gets squirreled away in the basement of your psyche might come back to haunt you. Trauma is stored in your body memory, creating potential for dis-ease until it is cleared in a healthy way. Given how each day, each moment, and each interaction surrounding your loss may be laden with intense emotion, taking time to revisit the experience with new eyes can be powerfully illuminating. Spilling your guts onto the page can be cathartic and transforming. Your journal awaits you, whether you choose to use the prompts in the workbook or free-writing for personal exploration. Consider unburdening yourself into your very own, private, journal.

LEGACY STORY: EDIE'S WRITING

I sat with Edie, an avid journal keeper, writer, friend, and colleague. She's a wise elder, now in her eighties. I wanted to learn how writing helped her grapple, grow, and ultimately transform the sudden death of her son, Jonathan, from grief to gratitude. Writing was a trusted companion on her path. His death was a devastation, initially categorized as a suicide. It unraveled Edie in every way, as a mother and as a person, tearing her identity to bits. Eventually that suicidal assessment was changed. But her journey through grief before and after that was fraught. She tells me that over the decades, she's come to understand the deeper meaning beneath her trauma. She said, "I stayed with journaling, writing, and re-experiencing everything." She told me this was what helped her through, and that one of the gifts of journaling was the container it provided. That was where she recounted the moments that helped her along the way. She documented one that sealed something "deeply important" into her consciousness. She woke up in the middle of the night, startled wide awake, sweating and hot. She looked out over the bay and saw Jonathan's face filling the sky. "He was there," she said, "as sure as I was alive." Edie heard his voice saying, "I loved you . . . I love you." This gave her certainty in "the quality that we call soul, essence, or life force." Edie said that this essential quality is something that endures, through light or energy or as part of the cosmos. Writing about the experience while it was fresh and visceral helped her hold true to its power. She called that power a gift amid her sorrow, a thread tangibly connecting her to the "Mystery." After seventeen years of sorting and sifting through her story, Edie still treasures this gold.

Themes about mystery and soul essence became one of the themes in the book she eventually wrote: *Light in Blue Shadows: A Journey from Grief to Gratitude*. As we cozied deeper into Edie's couch, with light streaming in the bay windows, she talked about waves of grief accompanied by "waves of completion" that came from her journaling. "That," she said, "helped put my emotions in order long before I conceived of writing a book." Writing, according to Edie, is a way to gather courage and strength. And peace. You don't need to write a book, but her words about free-writing as a way of putting your stories in order are wise.

Edie is still mining the gold in her story through journaling. When she writes about her loss, she finds new meaning in her stories. I love that at eighty-something, Edie sees her journey as a fluid, continued inquiry. Twenty-four years after Jonathan's death, Edie sometimes awakens at 4:30 in the morning, revisited by questions. She says that's the agony of being a parent to a no-longer-living son. She's learned to accept this suffering as a part of the human condition. On one of those 4:30-in-the-morning wake-ups, Edie began writing again. She reflected on when she first heard the news of Jonathan's death. She described the feeling of her body dissolving, saying she "felt this huge spaciousness" and the sensation of floating on the ceiling. As she journaled, Edie made a powerful connection about her ability to leave her body. As she wrote, she realized that she had learned to do this when she was born six weeks early. It's a quality she's had her whole life. Having spent the first month of her life in an incubator, Edie realized that she reached for the light outside her glass enclosure, psychically leaving her tiny three-pound body. Radiance became her refuge. While journaling she re-membered this capacity to disengage her soul from her body. It saved her life then and saved her again when Jonathan died.

Journaling illuminated Edie's understanding that her life was framed by bookends, traumatic birth on one end and traumatic death on the other. Both experiences infused with light. Her process reminds us that healing happens in layers, and that revelations evolve. Light was, and is, Edie's salvation. As the streaming sunlight in Edie's living room dimmed, we sat quietly. She said, "I realized that all of this is part of my karmic journey. Bringing consciousness to what we call birth and death. How a soul comes into the body and leaves. This awareness is a privilege." Through writing, Edie found her thread—the one we must all hold tightly to keep from getting lost. It links her most traumatic experiences to an inspirational purpose for being alive.

Edie's book, *Light in Blue Shadows*, has touched people around the world. While she didn't start out to write a book, it's won three national awards. Many have written to tell her how much it helped them in their grief. You can learn more about it and listen to Edie's readings on her website: edie.hartshorne.net.

Chapter Ten
LANGUAGE OF SOUL

The rich and multi-textured language of soul is strong medicine. It leads us deeper into our hearts, bridging our conscious mind and unconscious depth. Soul is always speaking. Yet, we must learn its vocabulary in order to hear its quiet but constant voice. We do this by developing the ears of our deepest selves, listening closely for our own unique dialect. And, by shifting our attention to its right-brained, word-free communication. For some of us, it presses into our awareness through synchronicity, imagination, metaphor, or somatic (body) experience. Many people hear the voice of soul most clearly in the wholeness of nature. For others, the conversation may be explored through intuition, dreams, feelings, or ceremonial practices. Whatever your favorite form of contemplating inner wisdom, soul language bypasses the ordinary speech of our left brain. These symbolic conversations connect us to our deeper psyche, where healing happens. This is soulwork.

I think of the deep psyche as the lower part of a giant iceberg. The tip is our known self, an outer identity, who we *think* we are. It's our everyday, functioning self. But, as we saw with the sinking of the Titanic, the hidden portion has a bigger impact. Symbolic of the deep unconscious, its invisible-to-the-naked-eye force shapes who we are. It has more power to heal or to harm us. If we pay attention to the hidden-from-view self, it will not destroy us. If ignored, it has potential to wreak havoc. Disease, addictions, or unconstrained habits are symptoms of the power of the deep unconscious to control our lives. On an awakened grief path, knowing that the unconscious carries more power than our conscious mind gives us an imperative: learn to speak its language in order to gain access to your deeper psyche. There is a wellspring of wisdom there waiting for you.

Soulwork engenders powerful healing. It's a dynamic, living, evolving process of symbolic soul-speak. The letter I wrote to Queen Persephone in the Underworld, and the ceremony of tossing my collaged casket into the metaphorical River Styx, is an example of soulwork. Through creativity and symbolism, I was speaking in the language of my soul. Engaging in conversations with nature gave me rest when I was grief-weary. I made slide shows and altars that told stories of my people. They were filled with images that had special meaning to me. These imaginal processes were soulwork, my deepest soul talking, helping me walk the road to healing. Your soul wants you to hear its voice. Bridging the right and left sides of your brain is essential for that to happen. Listening, thinking, and reflecting in the foreign tongue of soul-speak, just like the deep writing in your journal, will help you dig into your alchemical pot, wherein lies your inner gold.

LEGACY STORY: HEIDI'S SOULWORK

Back before Lois died, soul-speak was a primary form of exploration in my private counseling practice. Heidi was my client, grappling with the loss of her marriage. Her husband had barely moved out of their apartment when her father died unexpectedly. It was almost to the day of her mom's sudden death, eighteen years earlier. A new loss often restimulates past ones. For Heidi this was true. With unfinished mourning for her mother surfacing, Heidi sunk into her pain, coalescing three losses into one intense bundle of grief. She and I met to recount her story when I began this project. Heidi remembered that as she grieved, she learned to listen to the voice of her soul. The soulwork, she says now, was deeply comforting.

Her first soul encounter happened in the neighborhood where she was raised. Running was a ritual that bound Heidi to her dad. They often ran from their home to the family cemetery plot and back again, a ritual punctuated by a vignette they repeated each time. Rounding a corner on the way home, Heidi, the ever-dutiful daughter, would check in, saying, "Hey Dad, you okay?" The moment he answered yes, Heidi slipped into high gear, leaving him in her dust. She waved over her shoulder as he laughingly tried to keep up.

When Heidi went to her hometown for the funeral, she put on her old, familiar running shoes and ran their route to the family grave site, where her dad would soon be buried. Heidi chuckled as she described what happened next. "Before turning back, I tightened both my shoelaces as I always did. When I got to our same spot, I stopped, looked into the sky, and said out loud, "Hey Dad, how ya' doin'?" I looked down and both my shoes were untied. Turning back to the sky, I shook my hand and shouted over my shoulder, "You shit!" That's when Heidi realized he would always be there for her. Apparently, that meant he could still play practical jokes and make her laugh. The grief didn't go away, but trusting in a connection between seen and unseen worlds shifted her focus of attention. Her sorrow expanded slightly, making room for wonder.

When she returned home to Oakland, Heidi kept running, training for the Chicago marathon. Her favorite route included streets similar to her hometown neighborhood. Every time she ran, tears flowed. For five months, she ran and cried. Every day. She cried for her dad, her mom, and her marriage. Heidi told me that when her mom died, she didn't really feel it. Now she could do nothing but feel. Our bodies carry our lived experiences in their cells. Getting into our bodies moves blocked energy, releasing stagnant emotions. Embodiment is a grounding and stabilizing practice. The more Heidi ran, the more embodied she became and the more she grieved. Day by day, when she needed to connect with herself and her Ancestors, Heidi ran. It was her soulwork.

Heidi joined me on an Earth Wisdom retreat in the vast desert landscape of Joshua Tree National Park, where she experienced a second soul encounter. That weekend heralded barely a month after her father's death and the anniversary of her mother's, along with the finality of Heidi's divorce. She was immobilized by grief, unable to leave her tent to wander on a dream walk into the labyrinthine boulders surrounding our campsite. With no capacity to move, Heidi lay on the floor, sobbing into the earth beneath the nylon floor of her tent. With her tears, she let go of everything: her parents, her marriage, and her old self. She felt as if she had no choice but to sacrifice everything. Giving her grief to the earth was Heidi's holy surrender. The earth soaked up her tears and the old Heidi died as nature held her in its embrace. When she woke the next day, Heidi emerged like a newborn. Released, renewed, and cleansed by her connection with the ground. She put on running shoes and ran through the early morning desert. The world looked different. The day before, it had been nothing more than sand. But now Heidi had fresh eyes. Everything was brighter. Greener. Clearer. Her surrender to death was deep soulwork. Having hollowed herself out on that unfamiliar desert floor, she opened space for something else, equally unfamiliar, to enter. When Heidi lay down for a rest under a bush, she saw light shining on tiny yellow flowers. As she looked upward, a radiance appeared to illuminate the bush, the flowers, and her. Trying to describe the moment, Heidi said, "It was . . . I don't really have words for this . . . it was like spiritual light streaming in. The light was saying: Pay Attention! Look! It's right here. Beauty is all around you." Nature answered Heidi's soul lament with its glistening beauty.

This is what happens when we surrender our grief to something larger than ourselves. The wholeness of the natural world takes us to the core of who we are. It gives us access to the heart of soul-speak. It happened for Heidi and it can happen for you, too. Nature is there for you whenever you need it. The soulwork practices for engaging in nature, in the Stepping Stones workbook, will guide you in practices for tapping that wisdom.

Heidi's focus on beauty was seeded in her soul that day. When she returned home, she tended her soul and her grief by baking. Her dad was a baker. His dad was a baker. His brother was a baker. The whole clan, including Heidi, worked at the family bakery. Heidi dusted off a few old recipes and started making cookies. Nineteen years later, she bakes nearly twenty thousand Christmas cookies annually. She refines recipes, finds better butter than we can buy in grocery stores, and makes fourteen different kinds of cookies. Every single year. For each of eighty families around the United States, she bags fifteen to twenty of each tiny cookie variety into fourteen sparkling cellophane packages. Then each bag is nestled into a pouch, a scarf, or a recycled find that tickles Heidi's fancy. That bundle is tucked into a box that she then delivers (by hand or mail). I've received a hand-addressed box of Heidi's cookies for almost twenty years. I've helped dip butter cookies in chocolate on an early autumn Sunday afternoon. But that doesn't compare with being one of Heidi's cookie-packing elves on a chilly December night with a glass of mulled wine near to hand. Heidi says that she never knows what's going to happen at these cookie-packing parties. It ranges from a wine-infused teasing jag to a women's therapy session. What she does know is that the cookies create a space for people to connect. "There is this sweetness that surrounds the whole thing. It's not about the cookies. It's about belonging to each other." Cookies and community are Heidi's living legacy now. She turned grief and love for her Ancestors into a mission of sweetness, changing the world, one cookie at a time. If she can find purpose in that, you can find your mission too.

Chapter Eleven
THE MAP

It's been ten years since I went through the initiation of being disassembled and reassembled into a new form. I am grateful for all of it. As you know, I live in Oregon instead of California, where I am steward to Spirit of Resh Foundation and the Sanctuary at Rainbow Ridge. I support grievers in transforming their wounds into gifts and I collaborate creatively with colleagues whose losses fertilize their lives and work. The abundant richness of these relationships feeds me daily. Once, on the way to meet a friend, I mulled over my own journey through grief. Suddenly the map of my initiation became clear. In that moment of spontaneous illumination, a precise path of *Story*, *Reflection*, *Vision*, and *Action* revealed itself to me. These words define the Standing Stones that lie ahead, guiding sentinels on the Stepping Stone footpath of loss to legacy.

Story: I told my story again and again, in speaking, writing, and imagery. I made slide shows and collages that honored each person who died. I built altars, indoors and out, full of photos and memorabilia that recounted my connections with each person. I lit candles in remembrance of the fullness of their lives. These imagery stories were soothing to my hurting soul. The visual forms comforted me; gazing at them kept my people vitally alive in my heart and mind. I shared every form of story with anyone who would look or listen. This telling and retelling led me to remember not just who *they* were but who *I am*: a woman of purpose, grace, kindness and openhearted generosity. It was more than recalling memories; I was putting back together what had been broken inside me. I saw beauty at the core of each of us. No matter what had shattered, it was now restored. Love became my new story. The Story Standing Stone chapter is where your story will also evolve.

Reflection: I spent copious time in reflective rest, excavating all I'd learned from each beloved who died. I pondered the profound experience of midwifing Lois through death, witnessing that final breath. I explored how my family faced their illnesses. Their surrender and tenacity. I examined the roles we each played in our family story, digging into far more than the year of death. I replayed conflicts and assessed my part in them. I unearthed childhood wounds that generated my habitual attitudes of control. I found that what once excited me no longer did. I recalled my love of nature. I visualized a slower, kinder, quieter life. I accepted Aunt Myrtle's imperatives about a place calling to me, and being patient. As I scoured myself, my soul strengthened just as a broken bone knits itself back, fused more solidly from its once broken vulnerability. The Reflection Standing Stone chapter is where you will dig deep and mine for your inner gold.

Vision: My inner visions brewed. I imagined how the world would change if our culture accepted death instead of sweeping it under the rug like something to fear. Like something essential, denied. New ideas flourished about how life is enhanced when we accept death. We will all face death one day. Our own and others'. We can bury that reality. We can let it shatter us. Or we can embrace its inevitability. Our birth is celebrated as a grand entrance to life. Why do we not equally honor our exit as a precious departure? My ideas about bringing death out of the closet grew urgent. A vision of my new life and a revised approach to facing illness, death, and mourning began to coalesce. Who I wanted to be, where I wanted to live, and what I wanted to put my energy toward, re-formed into my new-normal. The Vision Standing Stone chapter is where you will begin to craft your more-than-a-new-normal life.

Action: Feeling excitement for life and a focal point for my energy was uplifting. I consciously stripped away unhealthy attitudes. I adopted principles of kindness and exercised compassion. I took steps forward. The seeds brewing in my imagination came into daylight. Collaboration became a key component of every aspect of my life. Personally *and* professionally. I founded Spirit of Resh Foundation with Sally. I took action, sitting at my keyboard every day, turning my stories, reflections, and visions into a book. I applied for grants and received one to usher *Two Rare Birds* into the world.

Then, with Seth, I pulled up my Oakland roots and moved to a new state. I started living a life I could barely imagine while Lois was alive. We created our sanctuary. It's where I feel her presence in everything I do. All that I have received from her, in both her life and her death, is part of me now. This life in Applegate Valley, Oregon, is Lois's legacy to me. The Action Standing Stone chapter is where you, too, will bring your living legacy alive.

Nearly five years later I am still growing into my new life, building my community and honoring my life mission. As I write, my Ancestor altar sits at my back. I talk to my people there and listen for their guidance in return. They are always with me, anchors on my unfolding journey. We are not alone on this path. Many others tread its ground in front of and behind us, in a long line of grievers. We walk together on this avenue of mourning, sometimes leading the way, other times following. With tears in our eyes, we see one another, sometimes trudging, other times skipping along the Stepping Stones. Each Standing Stone holds the energies of those who came before. Just as the mythic standing stones of Glastonbury Tor and Stonehenge hold mystery and wonder, these Standing Stones of *Story*, *Reflection*, *Vision*, and *Action* hold the pattern of your invisible thread of transformation. Their majestic presence awaits you.

Section Three

THE STONES WORKBOOK

Chapter Twelve
WELCOME TO YOUR STEPPING STONE PATH

Welcome to your Stepping Stone path of healing and transformation. Trekking from Stone to Stone is to follow the trail of the Loss to Legacy map. You can trust the map, even if you feel lost or scared. It *will* take you to the healing side of your passage. The four cornerstones of the map, *Story*, *Reflection*, *Vision*, and *Action*, are called Standing Stones. Like the pre-historic boulders of the iconic landmark, Stonehenge, they hold power, offering soulwork practices and exercises. Two Stepping Stones connect each Standing Stone, leading you along a well-marked trail of healing. Each of these Stepping Stones offer a worksheet followed by two journals. "My Journal" is a lined page for responses to suggested writing prompts. "My Imagery Journal" has blank pages for documenting your soulwork in images and photographs. Each one is designed to focus your inner exploration through the lens of that particular Stepping Stone.

In the Standing Stones, soulwork plays a big role. Engaging with nature, building altars, contemplative practices, and dreamwork are some of the practices you are invited to explore. They engage you in soul-speak, awakening or deepening your inner guidance. Soul-speak comes through feelings, sensation, intuition, and creativity. It comes when you release your everyday, ordinary point of view in favor of opening your imaginative, wild self. You know this place. When the metaphors of a poem resonate or music reverberates through your body, evoking heart-swelling emotions, your soul is speaking. When you sit quietly in nature and clarity floats to the surface, your soul is speaking. When inner wisdom arrives through serendipity or uncanny coincidence, this is your soul communicating with you. Suspending judgment and releasing your inner skeptic develops your capacity to communicate in soul-speak. Invite your imagination to wander. That is the foundation of all soul language.

In the Stepping Stones, each worksheet focuses on a specific theme, followed by writing prompts, suggested journaling questions, and imagery exercises. They support you in exploring that content more fully, helping you to rediscover your Self. You can include anything. Your person, your job, your role. Anything you've lost. If you feel remorse, regret, or guilt for any reason, you can let it fall out onto the page. If there is something you wish you had said, give that voice to writing. Or paste images torn or cut from magazines that express that wish. You can rage and lament and complain and scream in your journals. No one will tell you to pull it together. You can express relief, release, and feelings of freedom. No one will tell you those emotions are inappropriate. Whatever you write about, teasing apart your thoughts helps you know yourself in a new way. This is writing to heal, to unravel, to discover. Let go of your inner editor; there is no good or bad writing when it's for this purpose. Whatever you think, feel, or want, you can use crayon, color, or paint to lay yourself onto the page. These are words or images to reflect you to yourself. Release the art critic; this is solely about revealing your inner world in a way that helps you to see it in a concrete form. Whichever journal calls to you, let tears fall onto the page or your pen rip the paper. Write until the writing *writes you*. Paste images that speak to your soul. You will discover things about yourself, life, death, and everything in between with new clarity and understanding.

Take your time following the path as it's laid out, rather than jumping willy-nilly from Stone to Stone. I recognize that some of you, like me, a tried-and-true rule breaker, are likely to blaze your own trail through them. To you I say, trust yourself! Either way, I encourage you to be bold and to give it *all* a try. You are welcome to pick and choose how, what, and when you explore each of the practices offered here. Their purpose is to nourish and support you. Then, if the shoe don't fit, just toss it away and walk on! Take your time. If you find the tasks overwhelming, remind yourself to engage with them one at a time. Choose what speaks most to you. Remember, you have all the time you need. I invite you to follow my great aunt Myrtle's advice to be patient. I pass her wisdom to you, reminding you to trust that you have a mission ahead. Don't try to figure it out just yet. Whether it is big or small, it will become clear when the time is right. I had my own challenges with patience, but her guidance is sound. Find the process and practices that inspire you to say your very own *Yes!*

Chapter Thirteen
STORY STANDING STONE

In the *Story Stones*, telling your story of love and loss is the foundation of your meaning making. Too often, when it comes to stories of death, grief, or loss of any kind, I see people isolated within their own families and close friends. One phrase I've often heard from participants in every grief circle I've been privileged to lead, is: "I can tell this story only here. No one else understands." I feel deeply saddened when I hear those words, often accompanied by self-recriminations for not being positive, strong, or resilient enough. I'm stunned when they are followed by apologies for weeping, in grief circles of all places! I believe that cultural taboos encourage this shame, resulting in resistance to strong, powerful emotions. I can only shake my head in wonder at the emotion-denying culture we have become. But sharing your story, even within the pages of this workbook, is a profound and powerful way to start shattering the walls of that taboo.

STANDING STONE SOULWORK PRACTICES
STORY
Nature Practice

Deep gratitude to Animas Valley Institute for teaching me this model of conversations with nature. Thank you.

This practice is called a dream walk. Go outdoors, to a place of nature near your home or in the nearest park, beach, forest, or wild, open space. It can be anywhere. Even in your backyard, under a tree. You never know how your dream walk will unfold, but I've never heard a tale that was anything less than perfection, no matter what metaphoric symbolism arises. Let go of expectations in order to be fully present to whatever happens.

Get into Nature and Choose a Place

A local trail, a nearby park, or your backyard are a few options. Plan to set aside at least 60 minutes (more is ideal) for this soulwork practice. Do this practice by yourself. If you feel more comfortable going with a friend, prepare to do your practice solo while your friend waits or goes in another direction.

Prepare

Put everything you may need into a small backpack or bag for ease of movement. Be sure to bring water, a hat, sunscreen, and your journal and pen (and maybe a snack for after). You may want to bring a mat or low camp chair if you are away from comforts.

Cross the Threshold

When you arrive at the threshold of the natural environment, pause before entering. Take a breath.

Step into nature consciously, affirming that you are crossing into sacred space. Step across a threshold. This can be a line drawn in the earth, a log or stick, a creek or stream, or between two trees, shrubs, or rocks. Anything that marks the transition will do. State, out loud or quietly, "I am entering into the dreamtime." Once you enter, refrain from conversations with other humans, eating, or going into man-made shelters until your soulwork nature practice is completed.

Enter Sacred Ground

Invite a specific inquiry to gel in your mind. Repeat it to yourself to clarify what you are seeking. *See the following Story Stone Inquiry for suggestions.*

Story Stone Inquiry

Bring to mind who or what you have lost. Consider any strong feelings, questions, thoughts, or confusion that you carry about your loss or death of a loved one. What images or feelings have you been replaying in your heart and mind? What about them plagues you?

Form these feelings into a question. Carry that question as a request for wisdom or insight into your dream walk.

The Dream Walk

As you walk, pay attention to the natural world; notice where your attention is drawn. This may be anything: try not to have any preconceived notions. Follow any impulse, including a strong attraction or repulsion, toward a particular nature being. It may be large, small, or tiny. It may be touchable or unreachable. It may be inviting or scary. When something calls to you, however strongly, go to it. Consider everything: a tree, an animal, a ground hole, leaves, a boulder or rock, even birds or sky. In other words, anything.

Listening to Nature

When you arrive at whatever called you begin by telling nature, and this entity in particular, what you are seeking. Make a genuine offer to this being from your heart. (I like to pour a bit of water or offer praise for its beauty. Sometimes I leave a flower or stone, or express gratitude.) Feel free to sit with, stand in front of, lie down with, or touch this nature being. Prepare to have a soul-speak conversation. Respectfully introduce yourself, then speak your inquiry. Out loud is ideal. Whisper if you need to.

Listen. Nature communicates in soul-speak, not in ordinary language. Nature speaks quietly. Slow down to listen. Remember to listen for soul-speak through any feelings or insights that arise. Unbidden thoughts or metaphors are equally important. Sometimes words flow as if channeled. Trust that, and write them down. Take time to write about your experience in your journal before you leave. It's easier than you think to forget some of the wisdom offered back.

Note

If nothing specific calls to you, keep wandering and listening to the natural world around you. Nature speaks quietly and in the language of soul. Listen carefully. Metaphor, symbol, and feeling are all soul-speak.

You may want to choose a spot to sit, rest, gaze, or wonder what this place has to offer you. Jot down any thoughts, questions, emotions, insights, or impressions that come during your walkabout in nature.

The Return and Re-crossing the Threshold

When you feel complete, create closure with the nature beings that have offered guidance to you. Express gratitude out loud. You may want to make a closing offering. Cross a threshold back into ordinary time. Leave the dreamtime consciously, affirming that you are exiting sacred space. Step across a line drawn in the earth, over a log or stick, or between two trees, shrubs, or rocks, etc. This threshold doesn't need to be the same place you entered. State, out loud or quietly, "I am reentering *ordinary time.*"

Altar Practice

Create an altar, a sacred space dedicated to your loss or your beloved and your relationship with him, her, or it. This isn't intended for worship, rather as an offering, a hearth of homage to your loss. It can be a spot on a bookshelf in your living room, bedroom, or anywhere in your house. (I chose to open the sliding door to a closet in my office, a private and special space just for me, for my Ancestor altar.) The power of altar building may surprise you with its vitality. And you may surprise yourself with how engaging and creative it is to build one. You can add to or change it, any time you like. This will keep it vibrant and alive.

Create an Altar to Honor Your Loss and/or Ancestors

Keep this altar alive and vital by adding new pieces regularly. Make sure to keep it dusted. Add items that symbolize what you are feeling or experiencing. You can take items off and replace them with new pieces each week.

Choose a Special Spot, or Create One

Add a form of light (a candle, twinkle lights, a lamp, etc.) to the spot. Place photos that show the essence of your loss or loved one. Place memorabilia from your experiences, including your life together, or from your person's history. Consider adding pieces that symbolize the history of your lost job, identity, cultural mores, planetary wellness, or role. Representations of your loved one's lineage or heritage might also be a wonderful addition.

Your Altar Story

Once a week, ask yourself, what, if anything, is new? What do you want to add to symbolize that here? You may want to collect and add pieces of nature from your nature practice to symbolize your experience.

STEPPING STONE ONE
YOUR STORY

All stories begin long before loss occurs. Imagine the beginning of yours. Hold its breadth in your heart. Then break it down, categorizing the wide range of events into phases. Each phase is characterized by the unfolding of specific events, attributes, and qualities. For example, if your loss is from a pregnancy, the story began with your relationship to the other parent or your decision to become a single parent. If you're grieving a divorce, your story began during courtship and ends long past the finality of the separation. If your loss is related to cultural or planetary changes, when did your relationship with the earth and natural world begin? What was the first moment you became aware of the social fabric around you? My Stepping Stone story began with Lois's diagnosis and continues to this day. If I were redoing the Stepping Stones, I might choose to begin with our early childhood together. Wherever you choose to start your story, there are many ways to divide it into phases. There is no right way to do it. It's your journey and your story to tell.

Consider each phase of your story as a chapter unto itself, with its twists, turns, challenges, and blessings. Sectioning your story makes it easier to process and digest. All together, it's too big a mouthful to chew. Dividing it into chapters creates smaller bites. While the word "chapter" may imply that you're writing your story into a book, that's not the intention. It's a universal language used to divide stories into sections, and that's what I'm asking you to do.

In Stepping Stone One, come up with ten chapters (more or fewer than ten is okay, too) that describe your experience. Capture the essence of each one into a phrase that will become the title of that chapter. This will help you see your story more clearly. The words you choose can have a special meaning that only you understand. This is rich and connecting. Trust that your imagination has a wisdom of its own, laying out chapters in exactly the sequence you need right *now*. They form the foundation of your story today, and since you'll be using them in Stepping Stones to come, they will help you build upon it tomorrow.

STEPPING STONE ONE WORKSHEET
YOUR STORY

Create a Title for Each Phase of Your Story
Even though you aren't writing a book, we'll call each phase a chapter.

Preparation

Sit quietly. You may want to light a candle or play some quiet music. You might want to do this beside your altar. Take some deep breaths. Quiet your mind.

Imagination

Imagine that you could break your story into ten important phases. Each one is like a chapter in your whole story. Consider your relationship with your beloved—what or who you've lost. What is the quality or essential energy between you? Consider what happened that caused your ending or the death of your beloved. What were the key moments, turning points, or phases of that experience?

Break them down. Choose a phrase that captures each of those important moments or phases. Use words that have a special meaning for you. Remember to include moments after the death or ending occurred. Even months or years later.

Naming

Each phrase will become the title of a chapter of your story. Even though you aren't writing a book, using the metaphor of chapters works great! For each phase, what phrase captures it's essence? This is the title of a chapter of your story. Write it down.

My Sample

If I were to break my story into ten chapters right now, I would choose these titles:

Chapter 1. Oh No!

Chapter 2. The Universe is Made of Love

Chapter 3. I Miss Us

Chapter 4. Dave, Too?

Chapter 5. Happy Trails

Chapter 6. Patience of a Saint

Chapter 7. Death is Birth

Chapter 8. Visitations and Missives

Chapter 9. Two Rare Birds

Chapter 10. My Living Legacy: Resh Foundation

STEPPING STONE ONE
YOUR STORY WORKSHEET

Write your chapter titles here:

Chapter 1:_____

Chapter 2:_____

Chapter 3:_____

Chapter 4:_____

Chapter 5:_____

Chapter 6:_____

Chapter 7:_____

Chapter 8:_____

Chapter 9:_____

Chapter 10:_____

STEPPING STONE ONE JOURNAL

Explore the Chapters of Your Story

Preparation

Set your space for journaling. You might enjoy a cup of tea while you write. Ensure that you have a distraction-free environment. You may want to do this beside your altar. Release concerns about writing technique or grammar. Choose a favorite pen or sit comfortably at your computer. You might be more comfortable writing in short spurts. If this is you, set a timer for 10–15 minutes. If not, write for as long as you want. Think about your experiences or your people. Call them to heart and mind for a few moments. Begin when you are ready.

Journaling Tasks

Choose one of your chapters. Begin exploring the details of that part of your story. What were the key components of that time? What was hard, beautiful, poignant, or traumatic? Tell yourself the story in any language and with as much feeling as you can. Do this with as many chapters as you wish. It is likely to take many visits to your journal to flesh this out. You can do just one or two chapters now and come back to others later.

Other Journaling Options

Free-write about anything that you are currently experiencing related to your grief.
Some prompts:
What I remember today is . . .
*The qualities I loved the most about my beloved, job, role, marriage,
the earth or culture, old self, etc. are . . .*
I wish . . .
I am no longer . . .

MY JOURNAL

_____

_____

_____

_____

_____

_____

_____

_____

_____

_____

_____

_____

_____

_____

_____

_____

_____

_____

_____

_____

_____

_____

_____

_____

_____

_____

_____

_____

_____

_____

_____

_____

_____

_____

_____

STEPPING STONE ONE IMAGERY JOURNAL

Use Your Imagery Journal to Show Your Evolving Story

Draw or paste any images that symbolize the chapters of your story here. Or show your experiences from your soulwork practices by drawing or pasting images that symbolize those experiences. You may want to paste a photo of your altar here.

Imagery Tasks

Choose one of your chapters. What were the key components of that time? What was hard, beautiful, poignant, or traumatic? Show the story in images. You might want to create a collage of those experiences. Do this with as many chapters as you wish. You can paste photos of your beloved and/or of your relationship. Photos representing a loss other than people can go here, too.

You can also cut and paste magazine images that express what you are feeling right now and paste them here, or create a collage that incorporates any or all of the above.

Some more options for imagery tasks: Draw your feelings with crayons, Cray-pas, chalk, paint, or colored pens.

MY IMAGERY JOURNAL

MY IMAGERY JOURNAL

MY IMAGERY JOURNAL

MY IMAGERY JOURNAL

STEPPING STONE TWO
EXPANDING YOUR STORY

Every relationship we have is complex, filled with ups and downs, compromises and concessions, conflicts and resolutions. Hopefully these are balanced with generosity and graciousness. These light and dark aspects of the relationship with what or whom you've lost are like the warp and weft of a finely woven cloth that makes up the fabric of that relationship. Each chapter of your story is filled with these threads, multiple dimensions of color, tone, and texture. The idiosyncrasies, the good, the bad, the ugly, and the beautiful of your friend, lover, parent, sibling, mate, earth or culture, body, or role/sense of identity may now be something you miss longingly. They are the unique qualities that fill out the completeness of your story.

Stepping Stone Two is a simple way of naming those richly colored yarns, then exploring the intricate layers of your relationship and shared story. In this Stepping Stone, you will identify those threads by listing adjectives or descriptive phrases that express the nuances of each chapter. Using the secret language that you and your beloved shared gives this task special meaning. I know that when I write the uncommon phrases that my family and I shared, it's food for my spirit (and, I imagine, theirs, too). I believe that will be true for you, too. Consider words that define the passage, capture the essence of what the chapter represents, or describe your relationship. Include everything. Write your descriptive phrases on the worksheet; then explore each chapter more fully in your journals. Work with this Stepping Stone at your own pace. You have all the time you need.

STEPPING STONE TWO WORKSHEET
EXPANDING YOUR STORY

Write Descriptive Phrases or Adjectives to Flesh out Your Chapters

Preparation

Sit quietly. You may want to light a candle or play some quiet music. You might want to do this beside your altar. Take some deep breaths. Quiet your mind.

Imagination

Write the title of each chapter in its respective spot on the worksheet. Choose one chapter that you are ready to examine more closely. Close your eyes and invite yourself to fully remember the experiences that made up that chapter. Open to the range of emotions, attitudes, body sensations, or intuitions you felt during that time.

Naming

As words and descriptive phrases rise to the surface, write them into the blanks. Give yourself permission to experience anything previously unsaid, even to yourself. List five or more secret-language words or phrases describing that chapter. Repeat this process of imagination, remembrance, and naming with each chapter as you are ready.

My Sample

Some possible examples from my story:

Chapter 1: Oh No!

Stunned.
Scared.
Sad.
Alone. Numb.
What's in a sister?

Chapter 5: Happy Trails

The Triumvirate.
Dancing across the threshold.
Until we meet again . . .
Cowboy.
Innate Knowing.
Hugged by Spirit.

Chapter 7: Death is Birth

Kundalini meets Lamaze.
Relief.
Used-up body.
Awe. Beatific.
Push!

Chapter 9: Two Rare Birds

Beside the fireplace.
Forgiven. Humbled.
Who am I?
The first I'm hearing of it!

STEPPING STONE TWO
EXPANDING YOUR STORY WORKSHEET

Write descriptive phrases or adjectives to flesh out your chapters here:

Chapter 1: _____

_____

_____

_____

_____

_____

_____

Chapter 2: _____

_____

_____

_____

_____

_____

_____

Chapter 3: _____

_____

_____

_____

_____

_____

_____

Chapter 4: _____

_____

_____

_____

_____

_____

_____

Chapter 5: _____

_____

_____

_____

_____

_____

_____

Chapter 6: _____

_____

_____

_____

_____

_____

_____

Chapter 7: _____

_____

_____

_____

_____

_____

_____

Chapter 8: _____

_____

_____

_____

_____

_____

_____

Chapter 9:_____

_____

_____

_____

_____

_____

_____

Chapter 10: _____

_____

_____

_____

_____

_____

STEPPING STONE TWO JOURNAL

Write to Explore the Descriptive Phrases That Define Each Chapter

Journaling Preparation Reminders

Set your space for journaling. You might enjoy a cup of tea while you write. Ensure that you have a distraction-free environment. You may want to do this beside your altar. Release concerns about writing technique or grammar. Choose a favorite pen or sit comfortably at your computer. You might be more comfortable writing in short spurts—if this is you, set a timer for 10–15 minutes. Think about your experiences or your people. Call them to heart and mind for a few moments. Begin when you are ready.

Journaling Tasks

Explore what the adjectives or descriptive phrases of each chapter mean to you. Allow anything to surface from that chapter of your story, including any experiences you didn't understand at the time. Express any new feelings that come up as you write. Is there anything you haven't yet explored?

Other Journaling Options

Free-write about anything that you want to explore from your relationship with your beloved.
Some prompts:
Something that keeps surfacing is . . .
I wish we had talked about . . .
I want my beloved (boss, kid, old self, earth or culture, ex-friend or -lover, etc.) to know . . .

Begin Inviting Dreams Each Night

Keep a journal or paper beside your bed. Write down your dream immediately upon awakening. You don't need to do anything with these dreams. Just tracking them is important for now.
(*Stepping Stone Five offers tools for investigating their symbolism in more depth.*)

MY JOURNAL

_____

_____

_____

_____

_____

_____

_____

_____

_____

_____

_____

_____

_____

_____

_____

_____

_____

_____

_____

_____

_____

_____

_____

_____

STEPPING STONE TWO IMAGERY JOURNAL

Continue Using This Imagery Journal to Show Your Expanding Story

Remember, imagery is a way to become facile with imaginative soul-speak. Reminder: Partnerships between body, mind, and spirit can be expressed through imagery. Engaging with symbolic or imaginal language is like having a conversation with your soul.

Imagery Tasks

Show insights or feelings from your journal or soulwork practices in imagery. If your altar is evolving and changing, consider taking a photo to paste here. Also consider drawing pictures from your dreams. Show the dynamics between different characters or forces in the dream.

You may want to paste photos of your beloved and/or of your lost relationship (i.e., boss, kid, old self, the earth or culture, ex-spouse or friend, etc.), perhaps creating a collage of photos combined with magazine images that show how you are or were connected. You can cut out images from magazines that remind you of the dream and its sequences. Paste them in your imagery journal.

Some reminders of options for picture and imagery making: Draw your feelings with crayons, Cray-pas, chalk, paint, or colored pens. It can be abstract, and doesn't have to look like something or be artistic. Let your emotions pour through your fingers.

MY IMAGERY JOURNAL

MY IMAGERY JOURNAL

MY IMAGERY JOURNAL

MY IMAGERY JOURNAL

Chapter Fourteen
REFLECTION STANDING STONE

Reflection is a process of gathering information. It's how you digest your experiences and metabolize them into lessons learned, wisdom gained, and revelatory insights. The *Reflection Stones* are about opening to what you don't yet know in order to find a new perspective on your struggles and realities. Every life experience, no matter how wonderful or difficult, is a teaching moment. Seeing everything through that lens encourages understanding that the purpose of human life is to learn and grow. What did you learn about life from living in relationship with this person or situation for however long or short, or however wonderful or horrible? Extracting lessons learned requires curiosity and looking beneath the surface, beyond the obvious, and behind appearances. Looking back, peering at your known, familiar story, you'll need to take off any blinders or rose-colored glasses and replace them with a microscope. You'll benefit from a willingness to look at your pain, rage, love, connection, longing, horror, and sorrow through this new filter, one that changes what you see and how you relate to it. Mourning combined with exploring lessons learned reinforces a sacred truth: paradox, or the marriage of opposites, exists within everything. Conflicting feelings, attitudes, and beliefs can coexist. They are inextricable. Any opposing emotions you are undergoing, anger and love, trauma and beauty, sorrow and joy, or loss and gain are two sides of one coin of you and your loss. Whatever you find has the potential for bringing healing.

You may be like me. I prefer that Lois hadn't died. But since she did, finding a way to honor her life and our relationship by gathering what I learned is the next best thing. Writing in your journal about how you have been altered by your experience brings the possibility of seeing your story with new eyes. Perhaps you will articulate something you haven't realized before. Anger may give way to understanding, then compassion. Painful memories could be reframed until a new story takes shape. Remorse may awaken accountability or forgiveness. Sorrow can turn into gratitude. Acknowledging where you may be stuck or unchanged, alongside recognizing how you've grown, is equally meaningful. Wherever you are on the spectrum of post-trauma growth, consider making space for the possibility of finding pearls of wisdom in your reflections. Stepping Stones Three and Four are a path for sifting through the layers of your memories. As you begin looking for meaning in your traumas, you are building a bridge between your loss and its potential gain.

The Reflection Stones introduce a new soulwork practice: contemplation. Like mindful meditation, contemplation quiets the mind in the midst of everyday distractions, but the focus of attention, when in contemplation, is slightly different. Rather than seeking a meditative state of *no mind*, contemplation seeks a thoughtful state of *deep mind*. It's another form of soul-speak, inviting answers to your most sought-after questions. By listening to your depths rather than your everyday mind, you will learn to create an empathic inner atmosphere. I encourage your willingness to give all the soulwork practices your full attention. Even if they are foreign to you, give them a go. I trust that they will stimulate new perspectives, a key component of the reflection process.

STANDING STONE SOULWORK PRACTICES
REFLECTION
Nature Practice

Continued gratitude to Animas Valley Institute for teaching me this model
of conversations with nature. Thank you.

The dream walk is so valuable it bears repeating as often as possible. Remember, nature is whole. Since your body and the earth are made of the same matter, being in nature rebuilds your sense of wholeness. Continuing your soulwork nature practice regularly will sustain and develop your soul-speak skills. As you continue working with the Stepping Stones, new ideas, reflections, and questions will likely arise. Being in nature is ideal for accessing greater acumen in response to them!

Reminder: How to Take a Dream Walk in Nature

Get into Nature and Choose a Place

A local trail, a nearby park, your backyard, or someplace you and your beloved shared are a few options. Plan to set aside at least 60 minutes (more is ideal) for this soulwork practice. Do this practice by yourself. If you feel more comfortable going with a friend, prepare to do your practice solo while your friend waits or goes in another direction.

Prepare

Put everything you may need into a small a backpack or bag for ease of movement. Be sure to bring water, a hat, sunscreen, and your journal and pen (and maybe a snack for after). You may want to bring a mat or low camp chair if you are away from comforts.

Cross the Threshold

When you arrive at the threshold of the natural environment, take a pause before entering. Take a breath. Step into nature consciously, affirming that you are crossing into sacred space. Step across a threshold. This can be a line drawn in the earth, a log or stick, a creek or stream, or between two trees, shrubs, or rocks. Anything that marks the transition will do. State, out loud or quietly, "I am entering into the dreamtime." Once you enter, refrain from conversations with other humans, eating, or going into man-made shelters until your soulwork nature practice is completed.

Enter Sacred Ground

Invite a specific inquiry to gel in your mind. Repeat it to yourself to clarify what you are seeking.
(*See the following Reflection Stone Inquiry for suggestions.*)

Reflection Stone Inquiry

Bring to mind one of the chapters of your story. What did you learn (about yourself, your beloved, your past experiences with loss, or the world around you) during that phase of your story?

Reflect on the life you shared with your beloved, your ex, your family or kids, your job, the earth or culture, or whatever else you have lost. What did he, she, or it teach you about living? What did he, she, or it do that inspired you? What legacies did you receive from them? What does that teach you about living?

Form any of these reflections into a question.
Carry that question as a request for wisdom or insight into your dream walk.

The Dream Walk

As you walk, pay attention to the natural world; notice where your attention is drawn. This may be anything; try not to have any preconceived notions. Follow any impulse, including a strong attraction or repulsion, toward a particular nature being. It may be large, small, or tiny. It may be touchable or unreachable. It may be inviting or scary. When something calls you, go to it. Consider everything: a tree, an animal, a ground hole, leaves, a boulder or rock, even birds or sky. In other words, anything.

Listening to Nature

When you arrive at whatever called you begin by telling nature, and this entity in particular, what you are seeking. Make a genuine offer to this being from your heart. (I like to pour a bit of water or offer praise for its beauty. Sometimes I leave a flower or stone or express gratitude.) Feel free to sit with, stand in front of, lie down with, or touch this nature being. Prepare to have a soul-speak conversation. Respectfully introduce yourself; then speak your inquiry. Out loud is ideal. Whisper if you need to.

Listen. Nature communicates in soul-speak, not in ordinary language. Nature speaks quietly. Slow down to listen. Remember to listen for soul-speak through feelings or insights that arise. Unbidden thoughts or metaphors are equally important. Sometimes words flow as if channeled. Trust that and write them down. Take time to write about your experience in your journal before you leave. It's easier than you think to forget some of the wisdom offered back.

Note

If nothing specific calls to you, keep wandering and listen to the natural world around you. Nature speaks quietly and in the language of soul. Listen carefully. Metaphor, symbol, and feeling are all soul-speak.

You may want to choose a spot to sit, rest, gaze, or wonder what this place has to offer you. Jot down any thoughts, questions, emotions, insights, or impressions that come during your walkabout in nature.

The Return and Re-crossing the Threshold

When you feel complete, create closure with the nature beings that have offered guidance to you. Express gratitude out loud. You may want to make a closing offering. Cross a threshold back into ordinary time. Leave the dreamtime consciously, affirming that you are crossing out of sacred space. Step across a line drawn in the earth, over a log or stick, or between two trees, shrubs, or rocks, etc. This threshold doesn't need to be the same place you entered. State, out loud or quietly, "I am reentering ordinary time." If it feels appropriate, bring back symbolic nature objects to place on your altar.

Altar Practice

Continue Honoring Your Loss and/or Ancestors at Your Altar

Your altar evolves with you. Continuing to expand it keeps it vital and alive. Keep it fresh by visiting it daily and having an ongoing relationship with it. Add new pieces regularly.

Make sure to keep it dusted. Is there anything new you want to symbolize here? Consider bringing items from your nature practice to place on your altar. You may want to take a photo of your evolving altar and paste it in your imagery journal.

Contemplation Practice

Contemplation: An Imaginal, In-Your-Body Listening Practice

As you learn and practice this simple technique, it will invoke the voice of your wisdom. You will focus your full attention on an inquiry and invite a response to rise to the surface. This is how inner guidance becomes available. Whatever your question, contemplation is a way of exploring your evolving set of values and inner truth. Your contemplative practice needs to be carried out in a quiet, undisturbed place. It can be at home (perhaps beside your altar). Consider a place in nature or a church, synagogue, mosque, or retreat center. A sculpture garden at your local museum or perhaps in a comfy chair in a library may also work for you.

Prepare: Choose a Place

Get comfortable. Make sure you are warm or cool enough. Do you prefer to be indoors and contained, or outdoors, hearing sounds of life around you? Keep your journal and pen nearby so you can jot down any insights or responses to your inquiry. Some responses may come in images, feelings, bodily sensations, intuitions, or words. Trust whatever comes. Plan for a *minimum* of thirty minutes for this contemplation.

A Contemplation Inquiry: Choose Your Question

What have I learned through _____'s death?
What have I learned from what I once loved, but have lost?
How have I integrated these lessons? Are they part of my daily life?
Are there lessons I still need to work on integrating?
What values or qualities do I wish I were more able to embody?

The Contemplation

Quiet yourself. Take a breath, or three. Ask your question. Listen. Wait patiently for an answer. Try not to grasp for an answer. Trust that one will come from within the quiet. As your mind interferes, simply breathe and ask the question again. Take another breath. Continue waiting for an answer. Be still.

Remember, answers may come in images, feelings, sensation, intuition, or language and it often takes several rounds of asking your question before insight arises.

Answers take time. Be patient. Trust.

STEPPING STONE THREE
WHAT LIES BENEATH?

I imagine you've been changed by your experiences. In Stepping Stone Three, you'll articulate how you've changed and what you've learned. You'll need to look beneath the obvious, to what may be shadowy or hidden from you. Sometimes anger, remorse, regret, or other negatively perceived emotions, along with sadness and sorrow, arise. This is a natural and often essential part of the process. Other times people are surprised to find lighter aspects of their experiences. Whatever you find, these are powerful forces that give information about your true feelings. If any of these emotions come to the surface, what do they need from you? If they are directed toward yourself, God, or another person or people, what are they telling you? What is beneath the surface? These emotions are potent teachers if we are open to their lessons. Getting real with life, yourself, and what you are learning is a great antidote for suffering. It's helpful in this Stepping Stone to explore how you may be thinking differently about yourself, your life, your loved one who died, or any loss that you've experienced. This self-reflection opens a door to a new perspective, making it conscious by turning over the stone to see what lies beneath. In the upcoming worksheet, you will list each chapter and write out a few statements that describe what you were taught through your loss. Naming everything you've come to know, understand, and discover, from simple to profound, opens the doorway to more healing. Once you've named what you've learned, your journaling practices will give you a place to examine it in more depth.

STEPPING STONE THREE WORKSHEET
WHAT LIES BENEATH?
Turning Over the Stone

Reflect upon what your experiences have taught you about life, death, relationships, how to live, spirituality, what is important to you, etc.

Preparation

Sit quietly. You may want to light a candle or play some quiet music. You might want to do this beside your altar. Take some deep breaths. Quiet your mind.

Imagination

Choose one chapter to work with at a time. Connect with the phrases or adjectives that describe that chapter. Consider what those experiences taught you. What were the challenges? Is there anything you would do differently now?

Naming

Articulate the lessons. Capture those lessons in several phrases. Don't leave anything out, even if it seems obvious.

My Sample

Some possible examples from my story:

Chapter 1, titled "Oh No!" taught me that . . .

> In spite of conflict, love can survive.
> It's important to tell people that I love them.
> I need to be resilient.
> Family is really important to me.
> I don't like being left out.

Chapter 6, titled "Patience of a Saint," taught me that . . .

> In spite of trauma, angst, and fear, joy is possible.
> Every single moment of life is precious.
> Laughing instead of fighting changes everything.
> I don't always have to do things my own way.
> We are more alike than different.
> I need to remember what really matters.

STEPPING STONE THREE
WHAT LIES BENEATH WORKSHEET
Fill in the lessons learned from your experiences.

Chapter 1, titled _____, taught me that . . .

_____

_____

_____

_____

Chapter 2, titled _____, taught me that . . .

_____

_____

_____

_____

Chapter 3, titled _____, taught me that . . .

_____

_____

_____

_____

Chapter 4, titled _____, taught me that . . .

_____

_____

_____

_____

Chapter 5, titled _____, taught me that . . .

_____

_____

_____

_____

Chapter 6, titled _____, taught me that . . .

_____

_____

_____

_____

Chapter 7, titled _____, taught me that . . .

_____

_____

_____

Chapter 8, titled _____, taught me that . . .

_____

_____

_____

Chapter 9, titled _____, taught me that . . .

_____

_____

_____

_____

Chapter 10, titled _____, taught me that . . .

_____

_____

_____

_____

STEPPING STONE THREE JOURNAL

Write to explore what you've learned through your experiences.

Journaling Preparation Reminders
See chapter 13.

Journaling Tasks

Explore a particularly traumatic moment. Ask yourself what it taught you. Explore anything you learned from your person, job, identity, role, the earth or culture, etc. that died. Explore how, or whether, you are embodying the qualities or values he/she/it carried. Examine anything you learned from your encounter with death. What were the conditions surrounding the death? Did you learn something from that?

Write about realizations that have evolved since the death. Have you learned anything about culture or community? How did the nature of the death influence your relationship to it? Was the death sudden, prolonged, chosen, or accidental? Explore your understandings, both then and now. What have you learned?

Examine how your perspective may or may not have changed over time. What was your experience with medical or other professionals? With the medical system? Do you act differently toward yourself or others as a result of these experiences? Extract any life lessons that came from them. Knowing what you know now, is there anything you would do differently?

Other Journaling Options

Free-write about anything that you are currently experiencing related to what lies beneath.
Some prompts:

When I look beneath the surface, I see . . .

What's been hidden to me until now is . . .

What I want my beloved to know about me is . . .

What I want my boss, kid, old self, earth or culture, ex-friend or -lover, etc. to know about me is . . .

Continue Inviting Dreams Each Night

Keep a journal or paper beside your bed. Write down any dreams immediately upon awakening. You don't need to do anything with these dreams; just tracking them is important for now. Later, in Stepping Stone Five, you'll begin investigating their symbolism in more depth. If you have any insights from them now, write about that.

MY JOURNAL

_____

_____

_____

_____

_____

_____

_____

_____

_____

_____

_____

_____

_____

_____

_____

_____

_____

_____

_____

_____

_____

_____

_____

_____

_____

_____

_____

_____

_____

_____

_____

_____

_____

_____

_____

_____

_____

_____

_____

_____

_____

_____

_____

_____

_____

_____

_____

STEPPING STONE THREE IMAGERY JOURNAL

Use Your Imagery Journal to Explore What Lies Beneath

Draw or paste any images that symbolize what you are discovering. Add images that symbolize your experiences from your soulwork practices. You may want to take a photo of your altar and paste it here. Remember, soul-speak builds your relationship with the invisible part of the iceberg that influences you more than the visible tip. This is a powerful recipe for transformation, and it supports your continued healing.

Imagery Tasks

Consider choosing one or more of the following imagery tasks: Create images from your dreams. Find pictures in magazines and paste them together to show the dream dynamic. Draw or paste images of what has been revealed through journaling. Show what you have discovered beneath the surface of your loss or anything you've learned from your encounter with death.

What were the conditions surrounding the death? Did you learn something from that? If so, show that, along with how you have evolved since the death.

Consider making a collage that tells the story of your relationship with your beloved, job, marriage, the earth or culture, ex-friend or -lover, identity, boss, etc. Use photographs, interspersed with images collected from magazines, to symbolize the long body of that relationship. Show shared interests, values, or favorite places or experiences.

You can't go wrong with cutting and pasting magazine images that express what you are feeling right now. Create a collage—a tarot card—that symbolizes any lessons you are discovering in your story. Some tried-and-true options for imagery sources: Draw your feelings with crayons, Cray-pas, chalk, paint, or colored pens. Paste photos of your beloved and/or of your lost relationship (i.e., boss, kid, old self, the earth or culture, ex-spouse or -friend, etc.).

MY IMAGERY JOURNAL

MY IMAGERY JOURNAL

MY IMAGERY JOURNAL

MY IMAGERY JOURNAL

STEPPING STONE FOUR
MAKING MEANING

We will always grieve the deaths of our beloveds, sometimes more profoundly than other times. Finding even a kernel of meaning softens anguish that may surround your grief. Meaning doesn't eliminate pain, but it paves the way for purpose. The lessons learned through each chapter of your story are rich ground for meaning-making. They may have led you to change your attitudes or reaffirm values you've always carried. Maybe you have a belief that's always been just under the surface and has now risen to the top. Is there something you know now that you didn't before? Naming is an important precursor for making meaning from the meaninglessness of loss. If you've moved onto this Stepping Stone, you've named some lessons learned. That helps you lay claim to your experience and take ownership of what matters most to you. Stepping Stone Four is about turning your raw material into spun gold, harnessing your inner wisdom. You will explore what has become important to you as a result of your losses and articulate new values. You will search out the mundane or profound ways you think or act differently and name a new view of yourself, the world, or life itself. If you're uncertain whether you've learned anything, consider returning to Stepping Stone Three to reflect on what lies beneath. Re-explore the worksheets and spend more time with the journals and soulwork to see what else emerges. If you turned over the stone and found rich material, you are ripe for moving on to Stepping Stone Four.

STEPPING STONE FOUR WORKSHEET
MAKING MEANING

Develop Meaning from Lessons Learned

Explore beliefs, attitudes, ideals, or values that have changed as a result of what you've learned.

Preparation

Sit quietly. You may want to light a candle or play some quiet music. You might want to do this beside your altar. Take some deep breaths. Quiet your mind.

Imagination

Consider each chapter, one at a time. How have the lessons you learned changed you? What new ideals or values do you now carry as a result? Do you know or believe something you didn't before? What is that? Consider how you relate with yourself, others, or the world differently now. How does that reflect your attitudes or ethics?

Naming

Articulate any changed or reaffirmed beliefs, attitudes, values, or ideals. Own these as your wisdom gained.

My Sample

Some possible examples from my story:

Because of what I learned in my chapter 3, titled "I Miss Us,"
my changed or reaffirmed beliefs, attitudes, values, or ideals (wisdom gained) are

   Telling the truth, with compassion, is freeing.
   Seeing the world through another person's eyes is healing.
   It takes time to heal a relationship. But you have to start someplace—NOW.

Because of what I learned in my chapter 5, titled "Happy Trails,"
my changed or reaffirmed beliefs, attitudes, values or ideals (wisdom gained) are

   I believe that the veil between worlds is very thin.
   I trust that you are here even though I can't see you.

Because of what I learned in my chapter 9, titled "Two Rare Birds,"
my changed beliefs, attitudes, values, or ideals (wisdom gained) are

   Forgiveness is freeing.
   Being compassionate with myself and others makes a difference in my quality of life.
   Relationships thrive when I am more careful about how I communicate.
   Acceptance and letting go of grudges is both humbling and joyful.

STEPPING STONE FOUR
MAKING MEANING WORKSHEET

Fill in new perspectives, beliefs, values, attitudes, or ideals (wisdom gained) from lessons learned.

Because of what I learned in my chapter 1, titled _____,
my changed perspectives, beliefs, attitudes, values, or ideals (wisdom gained) are

_____

_____

_____

Because of what I learned in my chapter 2, titled _____,
my changed perspectives, beliefs, attitudes, values, or ideals (wisdom gained) are

_____

_____

_____

Because of what I learned in my chapter 3, titled _____,
my changed perspectives, beliefs, attitudes, values, or ideals (wisdom gained) are

_____

_____

_____

Because of what I learned in my chapter 4, titled _____,
my changed perspectives, beliefs, attitudes, values, or ideals (wisdom gained) are

_____

_____

_____

Because of what I learned in my chapter 5, titled _____,
my changed perspectives, beliefs, attitudes, values, or ideals (wisdom gained) are

_____

_____

_____

Because of what I learned in my chapter 6, titled _____,
my changed perspectives, beliefs, attitudes, values, or ideals (wisdom gained) are

_____

_____

_____

Because of what I learned in my chapter 7, titled _____,
my changed perspectives, beliefs, attitudes, values, or ideals (wisdom gained) are

_____

_____

_____

Because of what I learned in my chapter 8, titled _____,
my changed perspectives, beliefs, attitudes, values, or ideals (wisdom gained) are

_____

_____

_____

Because of what I learned in my chapter 9, titled _____,
my changed perspectives, beliefs, attitudes, values, or ideals (wisdom gained) are

_____

_____

_____

Because of what I learned in my chapter 10, titled _____,
my changed perspectives, beliefs, attitudes, values, or ideals (wisdom gained) are

_____

_____

_____

STEPPING STONE FOUR JOURNAL

Write to Explore Lessons Learned

Journaling Preparation Reminders

See chapter 13.

Journaling Tasks

Are you different today than before you took a descent into grief and loss? If so, examine how those changes (or any resistance you feel to them) are for better or for worse (or both). Wonder about how the two are interconnected. Is there anything you regret in your relationship with your beloved? If so, write about your remorse and what it's teaching you. Create a scenario and write about what you would do differently. Consider writing a letter to your loved one, job, marriage, earth or culture, self, or lost role, etc. Share what is in your heart now. Perhaps you can ask for wisdom or guidance about how to make meaning or find inner wisdom. Write a letter back to yourself from your loved one, job, marriage, self, the earth or culture, role, etc. Use a different colored pen. Has your grieving impacted your compassion quotient? Are you more or less compassionate than you were before the death? With yourself? With others?

Other Journaling Options

Free-write about anything that you are currently experiencing related
to finding meaning and wisdom.
Some prompts:
How I feel / What I think about looking for meaning in my loss is . . .
My part in resolving any "unfinished business" is . . .
The values, priorities, or activities of my beloved that I also care about are . . .
Forgiveness is . . .

MY JOURNAL

_____

_____

_____

_____

_____

_____

_____

_____

_____

_____

_____

_____

_____

_____

_____

_____

_____

_____

_____

_____

_____

_____

_____

_____

STEPPING STONE FOUR IMAGERY JOURNAL

Reveal the Meaning You Are Discovering in Your Story

Imagery Tasks

Show how you think, feel, or act differently than before your grief and loss. Explore what images express these changes, using them to capture wisdom that has grown in you since your loss. What do you know now that you didn't before? You can create a collage of images to show what you have learned about life or something that you would do differently. Reveal your part in resolving "unfinished business." Is forgiveness a part of that?

Get creative with how you work with imagery. Purchase some clay or Sculpey and make something to express your evolving emotions. Put it on your altar or in your garden. Take a photo and paste it here.

What happened on your dream walk? Tell that story in a collage. Or consider what has meaning for you today. Find an image that shows that meaning, either directly or indirectly, and paste it here.

Draw a picture of how you felt when you woke up from a dream. As always, if your altar is evolving and changing, take a photo and paste it here.

MY IMAGERY JOURNAL

MY IMAGERY JOURNAL

MY IMAGERY JOURNAL

MY IMAGERY JOURNAL

Chapter Fifteen
VISION STANDING STONE

Exploring the *Vision Stones* brings you to an apex. You've done the hard work of recounting your story. You've searched your heart to unearth lessons learned. And you've named meaning and wisdom grown from those lessons. Now you are at an important turning point: translating your wisdom into vision. Fully embodying our wisdom requires us to start giving it away. I call this *passing the torch*, because I love the image of light passing from one person to the next. Imagine this applied to the idea of legacy—each one of us passing our personal values and mores from one person to another and from one generation to the next. This takes meaning to a new level. Bringing lessons learned from our loss to our kids, closest friends, school, library, or local nonprofit is purposeful. It nourishes the soul and the community. It honors your past and your loved one. And it becomes the essence of your personal legacy.

It is time now to turn around and look ahead, envisioning a new life that's built on the foundation of the old, brick by brick. Choosing the principles by which we live, whether they come from the legacies we've been given or the ones we make from our own ethics, determines our own purposeful living. It truly *is* up to each one of us to make the most of the circumstances we're given by life. Choosing to live in ways that honor the life we've been given and the growth we've harvested through our traumas is rich and vital for ourselves and the world around us.

The beauty of passing that torch of wisdom and insight is this: giving is receiving. We're rejuvenated when we share our light. We're filled up. Paradoxically, we *have* to pass the torch of what we've gained if we are to keep it. As our new principles become part of our moral compass, *paying it forward* keeps us on the path of our own true north. The Vision Stones are about navigating by that star. They ask you to translate the values born from your loss into your unique vision of a living legacy. The Vision Stones ask: What matters to you now, and how do you share it? Who are you becoming now, and what does that look like? What are the hopes you have for your family and future? These are million-dollar questions and you must begin carrying them with you. Keep them on the back burner while you do errands. Simmer them while you work. Let them stew while you are with friends or family. Slow-cooking your vision, alongside the practices in these Stones, is how you transform your loss into legacy.

STANDING STONE SOULWORK PRACTICES
VISION

At this point in your path, you've become acquainted with three soulwork practices: the **dream walk**, your **altar**, and *contemplation*. Continuing these soulwork practices will provide consistency through the Vision Stones.

Nature Practice

Remember that wandering in nature invites us to drop more fully into our bodies, to slow down, be more reflective, and move into our own rhythms.
Reminder for dream-walk steps: See chapter 13.

Contemplation Practice

Remember that whatever your question, contemplation is a way of eliciting inner truth.
Reminder for contemplation practice steps: See chapter 14.

Vision Stone Inquiry for Engaging in Nature or Contemplation

What simple wisdom, grown from your loss, do you now carry? What is your vision for carrying that wisdom into the world? How does this relate to your Self, your family, and your community?

Is there a spiritual component to your new Self? If so, what is it—and how do you nourish it? How do you embody any new values or qualities that you care about now? How do you want to face your own mortality?

Altar Practice

Continue sitting with and building or revising your altar. Remember that keeping it alive bridges your mind, body, and soul. Pick objects or images that symbolize new insights received through your contemplation practice. Consider adding symbolic items from engaging in nature or contemplation to your altar.

Build on Your Altar to Honor Your Loss or Ancestors

Be sure to include objects that symbolize questions or inquiries (even confusion) as your evolving wisdom. Your altar is an expression of your inner Self—everything is welcome there.

Is there anything new you want to add? Keep bringing new items from your nature practice onto your altar.

Consider adding objects to symbolize insight gained from your contemplations.

Reminder: You may want to take a photo of your evolving altar and paste it in your imagery journal.

Dreamwork Practice

The Vision Stones introduce a new soulwork practice—**dreamwork shorthand**. It's a simple way for you to decipher your dream soul-speak. You've been invited to ask for dreams and to record them in your journal. Dreams are filled with characters, images, and interpersonal dynamics, each of them symbolic. Exploring them more closely will expand your fluency in the language of your soul. Asking for a dream to support your inquiry into a vision for your living legacy is another way to communicate in the language of soul. Here are the steps:

Dreamwork Shorthand: Step One

Write each dream in complete detail and in the present tense. Leave space between the lines for jotting notes during the next step of dreamwork shorthand. Writing and speaking the dream in present tense helps you slip back into the dream state and remember the dream more fully.

Dreamwork Shorthand: Step Two

Use a colored pen or pencil to underline each image, dynamic, or character in the dream. It's helpful to think of each one as symbolic. Be curious about each symbol and take care not to assume you already know what it means. A dream rarely comes to tell you what you already know. Being curious helps you be open to what you don't yet know.

Dreamwork Shorthand: Step Three

Consider your associations, correlations, impressions, or memories that are elicited by each underlined item. Write them down in the space you left between the lines, below the underlined words, or in the margins. This can be in your journal or on a separate page.

Dreamwork Shorthand: Step Four

Rewrite the dream on a new page, replacing each dream image or symbol with your associations.

My Sample

Here's an example of my dreamwork shorthand from a dream I had when I was finishing Two Rare Birds and envisioning Spirit of Resh Foundation. As you will see in the final step of this simple Dreamwork Shorthand technique, I could easily understand the meaning of my dream.

It affirmed the new life direction I was considering.. My soul was speaking to me and urging me forward. It solidified my idea of the connection between spirit and matter (the rainbow bridge) as an important part of my new life. It confirmed that it was time to emerge from the cocoon of my grief. Here's how I got there:

My Dreamwork Shorthand, Steps One and Two:
Write the dream and underline its symbols.

<u>Sally, Lois, Dave,</u> and I are standing before a <u>claw-foot bathtub</u> with <u>water</u> pouring into it and <u>flowing over the sides</u>. A magnificent, bigger-than-life, <u>multicolored butterfly</u> emerges from the waters. Lois turns to me and <u>gazes into my eyes with deep compassion</u>.

My Dreamwork Shorthand, Step Three:
Free-associate with each symbol.
Explore both personal and universal/archetypal associations.

<u>The characters: Sally, Lois and Dave</u>: These symbolic people are my (mostly dead) family. Lois and Dave are my Ancestors. Sally is one of my closest soul companions. Together we acted as spiritual guides to Lois as she was dying.

<u>The claw-foot bathtub</u>: I grew up with one. As a child, I often took playful bubble baths and later, as a teen, long, luxurious ones inside its deep vessel. My mom said that if I was unhappy, all she

needed to do was get some bubbles going, then plop me into it; later I would emerge full of joy. That tub was a place of restoration, peace, and emotional stability for the child of me and as an adolescent, throughout that powerful transformative life phase.

The overflowing water: I associate water with the essence of life, flow of emotions, and the ebb and flow of the deep unconscious. There is an abundance of this force in the dream. It is, seemingly, never-ending.

The multicolored butterfly: Butterflies emerge from a cocoon in which a caterpillar becomes mush, much like I was when Lois first died. They symbolize transformation, a new life born from the disintegration of the old. The multi-colors of the butterfly in my dream remind me of a rainbow and the idea of serving the rainbow bridge that my Ancestor suggested to me.

Lois's compassionate gaze: This love burning into me reminds me of the unconditional love, the fabric of the universe she talked about so often. It feels to me like she was offering something to me in her gaze, something beyond the physical, human realm, into a spiritual connection. With Lois gazing so penetratingly into me, I felt her visceral presence and that she would be with me, always.

My Dreamwork Shorthand, Step Four:
Rewrite the dream, replacing each image or character with your associations.

With my Ancestors and my soul guides beside me, I am standing before a place of restoration and peace, facing an abundantly overflowing essence of life that takes me to a place of joy. A giant transformation that is connected with the rainbow bridge is emerging from my deep unconscious. The unconditional love from my Ancestors goes beyond the physical; it's a spiritual connection that will be with me, always.

Work With Dreams to Develop Your Vision

Invite Your Dreams

Continue Inviting Dreams Each Night. Keep a journal or paper beside your bed. Write your dream immediately upon awakening.

Get Specific

Ask for dreams that help you craft your vision. Some possible questions to ask as you are falling asleep are: How do I translate _____ (the meaning you've named) into a vision for my life? What would honor _____'s life? What would honor the job, marriage, the earth or culture, old self or other loss and its past presence in my life? How can I carry out my own, unfolding, still evolving, legacy?

Use Dreamwork Shorthand to Explore the Messages in Your Dreams

Discover some surprising messages. Write the dream in detail, in the present tense, then underline each symbol. Free-associate to each underlined word and write your associations in the space between lines. Rewrite the dream by replacing the underlined words with your associations. Consider reading it out loud to hear your own symbolic language expressed.

Explore Past Dreams

Apply dreamwork shorthand techniques to each one.

Optional: Look for Emerging Themes

Put a series of past dreams together on one page. Treat these dreams as one whole, epic dream. Look for repeating symbols. Using the associative technique you learned in dreamwork shorthand, make intuitive leaps about the epic nature of your dream themes.

STEPPING STONE FIVE
ENVISIONING POSSIBILITIES

Exploring a vision for yourself is like gathering shells on a beach. All the pieces of your vision are already there. You've been naming them as lessons learned, values or attitudes of your loved one, and re-membered values from your soul. You've explored a revised relationship with life, death, loss, and love. Now, to envision possibilities for your living legacy, you are leaving the descent of winter behind as you enter into the rebirth of spring. It's a great time for brainstorming. Imagine wandering on the beach, picking and choosing among the many shells, picking up the ones that call to you. Envisioning possibilities that your mourning has washed onto your shore is a lot like that. There are many options, but only some of them will speak to you.

Let go of any fears you may have about change. Accept that you can move on *and* be true to what was *before*. Your vision is there. Open to it. Once you let it in, it will expand. It doesn't need to be big. It needs only to be authentic. Allow what is already inside you to surface. You've sat at the hearth of your own soul and found meaning in the Reflection Stones. In this fifth Stepping Stone, you're invited to envision possibilities for the reconfigured you. Your vision may not be as massive as mine. Nor does it need to be connected to death and dying. What's important is that your vision is *yours*, and that makes it sacred. For your vision to be true, it needs to emanate from inside you. It can't be forced, but it can be nurtured. Now it's time to nurture your vision into existence.

STEPPING STONE FIVE WORKSHEET
ENVISIONING POSSIBILITIES

What is Your Vision for Yourself?

Preparation

See chapter 13 for worksheet preparation reminders.

Imagination

Contemplate your vision for yourself before filling out this worksheet. Reconnect with the meaning you've named in each chapter. Translate that meaning into a vision for yourself. Reminder for contemplation practice: See chapter 14.

Naming

Articulate your vision in the worksheet below.

My Sample

Some possible examples from my story:

With the meaning I found in chapter 6, titled "Patience of a Saint," about how being fully present eliminates the need for patience, I envision enacting the belief that giving is receiving, and making time to slow down, and really "be with" people as wisdom to bring into my life.

With the meaning I found in chapter 7, titled "Death is Birth," about the need to honor death in the same way we honor birth, I envision accepting that death is a necessary and beautiful part of treating my life as precious (even the hard stuff) as wisdom to bring into my life.

STEPPING STONE FIVE
ENVISIONING POSSIBILITIES WORKSHEET
Describe your vision for yourself here:

With the meaning I found in my chapter 1, titled _____, about _____

_____, I envision _____

_____

as wisdom to bring into my life.

With the meaning I found in my chapter 2, titled _____, about _____

_____, I envision _____

_____

as wisdom to bring into my life.

With the meaning I found in my chapter 3, titled _____, about _____

_____, I envision _____

_____

as wisdom to bring into my life.

With the meaning I found in my chapter 4, titled _____, about _____

_____, I envision _____

_____

as wisdom to bring into my life.

With the meaning I found in my chapter 5, titled _____, about _____

_____, I envision _____

as wisdom to bring into my life.

With the meaning I found in my chapter 6, titled _____, about _____

_____, I envision _____

as wisdom to bring into my life.

With the meaning I found in my chapter 7, titled _____, about _____

_____, I envision _____

as wisdom to bring into my life.

With the meaning I found in my chapter 8, titled _____, about _____

_____, I envision _____

as wisdom to bring into my life.

With the meaning I found in my chapter 9, titled _____, about _____

_____, I envision _____

as wisdom to bring into my life.
With the meaning I found in my chapter 10, titled_____, about _____

_____, I envision _____

as wisdom to bring into my life.

STEPPING STONE FIVE JOURNAL

Write to Explore How the Wisdom You Have Gained Informs Your Vision

Journaling Preparation Reminders

See chapter 13.

Journaling Tasks

Who are you now? And who are you no longer? Explore the layers that have been shed. Who are you, really? What qualities or values of your loved one, job, marriage, old self, earth or culture, etc. do you most want to carry on? Consider what part of that past you still want to embody. Consider how s/he lived and what of that you that you want to embody. Imagine how you want your new life to look and what the daily actions are that would embody your changes. What is your vision for your inner life, going forward? Explore your hopes or intentions for developing or deepening your spiritual life.

Other Journaling Options

Free-write about anything that you are currently experiencing related to your vision for your life.
Some prompts:
Who I am, now, is . . .
What I've learned about my relationship with death is . . .
What I know now about healing is . . .

You might also want to explore your dreams. Think about every symbol in the dream as representing an aspect or part of you. Write about what that might mean.

MY JOURNAL

STEPPING STONE FIVE IMAGERY JOURNAL

Paste Images That Symbolize Your Vision for Yourself

Imagery Tasks

Make a vision collage of pictures (preferably no words). Don't think about it; just go by gut. If you feel vision-less, let the images that speak to you be your guide. Hold this question in mind: What do I envision for my life, now?

Peruse magazines (look in thrift stores for old copies of *National Geographic* or buy some magazines at a newsstand if you don't have any at home), as you keep repeating that question. This is like an embodied contemplation. Cut or tear out any images that bring a spark. Don't stop to read the articles. It's ideal to choose only images. (But if there are words you can't pass up, go for it.) Do this intuitively. Don't overthink; just do it. Keep turning the pages and moving forward without assessing what an image means. When you feel done, start placing the images on a large piece of tagboard. Move them around until they fit "just right." Glue them down.

When you are done, stand back and look at the collage as a whole. Consider it as if you are reading a dream. Consider the collage to be a story full of symbolism. What are the symbols or forces in this picture/word story? What does the interplay between images (and words) suggest to you about your own vision, possibilities, or callings. Consider the collage to be "greater than the sum of its parts." Notice how the images interact with each other. What story are they telling? Use this to explore your vision in more depth in your written journal.

Some tried-and-true options for your imagery journal: Paste pictures of any evolution with your altar. Add photos from your dream walks. Draw the feelings that came during a contemplation. Draw images from your dream. Consider taking a photo of the collage and pasting it into your imagery journal.

MY IMAGERY JOURNAL

MY IMAGERY JOURNAL

MY IMAGERY JOURNAL

MY IMAGERY JOURNAL

STEPPING STONE SIX
BUILDING PURPOSE

You've been reshaped. You've named a vision for yourself. Now it's time to imagine passing that vision to others. What do you want for your family? For your friends? What ideas or values do you want to awaken in the people around you? Is there anything you long for in your community? Or the larger culture? Stepping Stone Six asks you to give voice to any dreams you now have for the world you inhabit. Desires or aspirations grown from your loss and this Stepping Stone journey are the foundation of your purpose vision. Besides being an essential building block of your living legacy, living on purpose is revitalizing. And healing.

Purpose is immeasurable, rooted in your tiny insights and giant *aha's*. Shaped by everything you've lived, it's not defined by size but rather by dedication. Purpose fills you up. It's what you think about, first thing, upon awakening. It's what you can't help but focus on while you're driving, packing lunch, or watering your garden. It's what you offer the world because you can't not. Characterized by compassion and commitment, it doesn't matter whether your purpose is connected to vocation or avocation. It's only about the ripple effect of you, and all the ways you've changed, touching others. As the torch of wisdom grows from your loss, your purpose shimmers with light. Stepping Stone Six is about envisioning that radiant purpose.

STEPPING STONE SIX WORKSHEET
BUILDING PURPOSE

Name Your Hopes for Family, Friends, or Community

Preparation

See chapter 13 for worksheet preparation reminders.

Imagination

Contemplate your vision for the world around you before filling out this worksheet. Reconnect with your wisdom gained from each chapter of your story. Now consider what you want others to know. What do you want for your family? Your community?

Naming

Articulate your vision of what you want people to know or what you hope for in your community.

My Sample

Some possible examples from my story:

As a result of my loss, what I want other people to know is that there is more to life than what we see with our eyes.

As a result of my loss, what I hope for in my community is that, as people find meaning in loss, they create legacies that make a difference.

STEPPING STONE SIX
BUILDING PURPOSE WORKSHEET

Name the vision of what you wish to pass to others as a result of your loss.

As a result of my loss, what I want other people to know is_____

_____

_____

_____

As a result of my loss, what I hope for in my family is _____

_____

_____

_____

As a result of my loss, what I hope for in my community is_____

_____

_____

_____

STEPPING STONE SIX JOURNAL

Explore the Legacy You Hope to Leave in Your Own Wake

Journaling Preparation Reminders
See chapter 13.

Journaling Tasks

Explore your vision for your outer life, including yourself, your family, or your community. What are the gifts you have received that are most needed? What do you, uniquely, bring to life, your family, or your friends?

Explore the ideas, ethics, and values you envision for your family, for your friends, or for your extended community. What qualities or values of your loved one, marriage, the earth or culture, old self, etc. do you most want to carry on? What actions would demonstrate these qualities?

Write about transitioning from winter to spring, or the metaphor of tossing off your gray cloak of mourning. Are you ready? If not, what else is needed?

Other Journaling Options

Free-write about anything that you are currently experiencing related to your living legacy. You might also want to continue journaling about your dreams:
Some prompts:
What I feel committed to for the rest of my life is . . .
What I am no longer committed to for the rest of my life is . . .
What I've care about more than anything is . . .
The places in my community that need what I have to offer are . . .

You might also want to continue journaling about your dreams:

Dreamwork Reminders: Some Tips for Exploring Your Dreams

Think of your dreams as a snapshot of the state of your inner world. Consider that they might be a hint about building your vision right now. Imagine them as symbolic postcards sent from your soul.

Sometimes Ancestors talk through synchronicity or dreams. Are they coming to you in some way? If so, are they informing you about your vision? It's also fine not to make any particular meaning of their appearance. Appreciate their visit if that happens. Trust the images, even if you don't understand them. *If you aren't experiencing this, please don't judge your experience.*

Translate dream symbols into your imagery journal in any way that feels fun to you. Consider colorful crayons, collage, or even drawing stick figures or emojis.

MY JOURNAL

_____

_____

_____

_____

_____

_____

_____

_____

_____

_____

_____

_____

_____

_____

_____

_____

_____

_____

_____

_____

_____

_____

_____

_____

_____

_____

_____

_____

_____

_____

_____

_____

_____

_____

_____

STEPPING STONE SIX IMAGERY JOURNAL
What Do You Want to Pass On to Others?

Imagery Tasks

Show your vision here. Try buying a hunk of clay and sculpt your vision for your extended community into it. Place that symbolic clay work on your altar, take a photo, and paste it here. Or paste images that symbolize your vision for your community and the lives of people around you.

Consider making a collage that tells the story of what you want to pass to your family. Use photographs and images collected from magazines, and be sure to symbolize the shared interests, values, or favorite places or experiences from your loss. Include any images that symbolize your experiences from soulwork practices.

Explore brand new ways to concretize and embody your vision. You might want to purchase a piece of art that expresses the wisdom you've found in your story. Hang it prominently in your home.

As always, if your altar is evolving and changing, consider taking a photo and pasting it here.

MY IMAGERY JOURNAL

MY IMAGERY JOURNAL

MY IMAGERY JOURNAL

MY IMAGERY JOURNAL

Chapter Sixteen
ACTION STANDING STONE

I had a teacher once who repeated these words over and over: *See one. Do one. Teach one.* I've carried this principle throughout my life as I grew from one life stage to the next. To *see one* is to envision possibility for yourself. You completed this in the Vision Stones, discerning what matters most to you and crafting a vision for your life. To *do one* is to practice behaviors that are in accord with and support that vision. This *doing* is what you are exploring in these *Action Stones.* You will outline behaviors and actions that demonstrate your vision and then practice them in order to transform that vision into reality. Just as a pianist must practice scales so that her fingers can effortlessly find each key, you need to practice specific behaviors until they are an organic part of your nature. This process supports you in the final phase. To *teach one* is to carry out your living legacy as service to others. *Seeing* is the seed that was born of your reflection. *Doing* is the nurturing and growth of that seed into a lush plant, your vision of a living legacy. *Teaching* is the fruit of your harvest, carrying your wisdom into your world. Going beyond the idea of *teaching,* these Action Stones center on what I call your *giveaway.* In many Native American cultures, the ceremony of giveaway is to offer thanks or pay an honor toward something. It's a fitting term for service that honors the losses of our lives. Resting on the principle that giving is more sacred than receiving, "giveaway" suggests that service to the community offers riches back to the individual. Always. A society formed around service is healthy, whole, and balanced. Its wisdom is this: love begets more love until it circles around and feeds everyone it touches. What better way to immortalize the people or things you've loved and lost? Gathering your experiences and carrying them into the world as your giveaway is what the Action Stones are about. They ask you to identify simple actions that embody your giveaway and practice them until they become second nature. Then you will put everything these Stones have given you into a personal Legacy Mission Statement. This is your vow to yourself. I hope that you will carry it passionately and gracefully into your life. Welcome to spring.

STANDING STONE SOULWORK PRACTICES
ACTION

As you integrate soulwork practices into your lifestyle in a rhythm sustainable for you, they will become an ever-present tool for helping you connect with your soul. I leave it to you to strengthen your soulwork rhythms in your own way, much like the way a baby chick must peck her own way out of the egg in order to develop strong neck muscles.

Find a pattern that suits you for engaging with your inner world as you consciously step into an outer one focused on service. Engage in nature, contemplation, altar building and tending, and dreamwork in your own rhythm and timing as you explore how to bridge inner and outer practices.

Using soulwork practices to support your exploration into service, consider this **one** question:
What serves my rebirth, and my service to community, now?

Nature Practice
Reminder for dream-walk steps: See chapter 13.

Contemplation Practice
Reminder for contemplation practice steps: See chapter 13.

Dreamwork Practice
Reminder for dreamwork practice steps: See chapter 14.

STEPPING STONE SEVEN
PRACTICE, PRACTICE, PRACTICE

Carrying out a living legacy isn't a done deal. Our commitment to it must be continually renewed. This reality keeps us humble on our path of honoring our loss and remembering who we are and who we're becoming. Practice, enacting the same intention with a regular and repeated rhythm, helps us embrace our new identity. This focus and repetition is necessary if we are to ground our vision. It's one thing to contemplate the gifts from your grief; it's an entirely new diligence and pleasure to embody those ideals. Your loss revealed what really matters to you and you've named that in the Vision Stones. This Stepping Stone is about bringing those visions, one for your Self and another for your community, into reality. Practice is how you will do that. There are infinite ways to develop your own practices. Maybe you're committed to carrying out the qualities or values of the person you loved. Maybe you want to volunteer with an organization that matters to you. Perhaps lessons from caregiving, or watching someone take a last breath, have awakened insight or spiritual meaning. Whatever your vision is, a routine of behaviors, actions, or attitudes will get you there. It's time to start practicing.

In this Stepping Stone worksheet, you will consider what honors the life and death of your beloved, the marriage, old self, career, or other personal, cultural or planetary attributes you've lost. You will brainstorm behaviors or attitudes that will bring that to life. Then you will start practicing. Engage in these practices with your family. Do them in the grocery store, at work, and when you are playing. They are your soulwork now, as you take the language of your soul into the language of everyday. Fill your actions with self-love, forgiveness, consciousness, and all the grace you can muster. It's the least you can do for the fragile new you that is emerging.

STEPPING STONE SEVEN WORKSHEET
PRACTICE, PRACTICE, PRACTICE
Name the Actions That Express Your Wisdom and Vision

Preparation

See chapter 13 for worksheet preparation reminders.

Imagination

Brainstorm some actions that would express your wisdom and vision for your life and community.

Naming

Write a practice agreement to define how you will enact those actions.

My Sample

Some possible examples from my story:

Some actions that would express my living legacy are: Tell the people I care about that I love them; Listen with patience and compassion; Slow down in order to be present with myself and others; Let go more, and trust others; Create ceremonies that honor Ancestors.

A practice agreement I might write could be this: The actions that express my beliefs about spirit, my newfound wisdom about forgiveness, and/or my passion about accepting death as part of life will be to light a candle to my honor my Ancestors, do forgiveness meditations, spend more time in nature and contemplation, and take time to listen to others.

I promise myself to carry these out one time a day, for at least three days a week.

STEPPING STONE SEVEN
PRACTICE, PRACTICE, PRACTICE WORKSHEET

List the brainstorm of actions that express your beliefs, wisdom, or vision for your life and community.

Be BOLD! Write it down even if it's outlandish.
(You can decide later which actions you will choose to practice.)

_____

_____

_____

_____

_____

_____

_____

_____

_____

Now Write These Ideas into a Practice Statement

Consider practices that are personal and just for you. Consider any spiritual practices that will nourish your soul. Consider others that focus outward on service toward your community.

The actions that express _____, _____, and/or _____ will be _____, _____, and _____.

I promise myself to carry these out _____ times a day, for at least _____ days a week.

The actions that express _____, _____, and/or _____ will be _____, _____, and _____.

I promise myself to carry these out _____ times a day, for at least _____ days a week.

The actions that express _____, _____, and/or _____ will be _____, _____, and _____.

I promise myself to carry these out _____ times a day, for at least _____ days a week.

The actions that express _____, _____, and/or _____ will be _____, _____, and _____.

I promise myself to carry these out _____ times a day, for at least _____ days a week.

STEPPING STONE SEVEN JOURNAL

Write to Explore What You Will Do to Carry Out What You Have Received From Your Loss and/or From Your Ancestors

Journaling Preparation Reminders

See chapter 13.

Journaling Tasks

After practicing your actions in the world, reflect on how that practice impacted you and others. If you are engaging with any inner, spiritual practices, reflect on how they are impacting your relationship with others.

If you faced resistance and struggled to maintain your practices, explore what got in your way. What did you tell yourself about that? Consider what will enable you to recommit and stay accountable to yourself. Do you need to make any adjustments in your promise?

Reflect on the meaning of "legacy" to you. Consider all that you've learned and define what it means to live a legacy.

Other Journaling Options

Free-write as desired. Some questions to consider:
What is your unique giveaway?
What simple, daily behaviors embody your vision?
What community action(s) would express your inner principles?

MY JOURNAL

_____

_____

_____

_____

_____

_____

_____

_____

_____

_____

_____

_____

_____

_____

_____

_____

_____

_____

_____

_____

_____

_____

STEPPING STONE SEVEN IMAGERY JOURNAL

Show What It's Like to Practice New Actions

Imagery Tasks

Paste images that symbolize your vision for your community and the lives of people around you.

Show your practice statement in pictures. Express what it feels like to engage with your practices (or show any resistance you are encountering). Paste images that symbolically represent your experience of how your practice impacts or influences others.

As always, continue adding any images that symbolize your experiences from soulwork practices. Paste pictures of any evolution of your altar. Add photos from your dream walks. Draw feelings that came during a contemplation or from a dream.

MY IMAGERY JOURNAL

MY IMAGERY JOURNAL

MY IMAGERY JOURNAL

MY IMAGERY JOURNAL

STEPPING STONE EIGHT
THE GIVEAWAY

Each of us has our own unique giveaway, actions that embody our wisdom. This giveaway is an act of *seva*, a sanskrit word meaning selfless service. To perform seva is to offer oneself freely, until giving becomes its own reward. When we are acting selflessly, we feel gratitude for the opportunity to be of service. Providing care, seeing another's need and answering it, alleviating suffering in word or deed: these are acts of seva. Doing them releases endorphins and we feel their rush of connection. By turning what is close to your heart into seva, you are creating a living legacy. Seva is giveaway in the highest meaning of the word.

Stepping Stone Eight, the final step on this path, asks you to create a personal Legacy Mission Statement. It's a sacred vow to yourself and to all you've lost. It will guide you through your one-day-at-a-time life. It will usher you forward, into the future you choose. You may revise this statement throughout your life. Checking in ensures you hold to your own ever-evolving mission. Before writing it down, contemplate all that the Stepping Stones have awakened or deepened in you. Make a ritual of the commitment you are about to make. You might like to light a candle. Maybe you will frame it to hang above your altar. Or you may simply write it down, speak it out loud, and place it where you can see it every day. Whatever you do, remember to keep your mission statement in the forefront of your awareness. It's the essence of what you hope to leave in your own wake. And it honors your loss and everything you have learned from it.

STEPPING STONE EIGHT WORKSHEET
THE GIVEAWAY

Write Your Personal Legacy Mission Statement

Preparation

Sit quietly.

Imagination

Consider how you want to live in remembrance of your losses.

Naming

Use any or all of the following formats to write your own personal legacy statement. Please take a few deep breaths with eyes closed before you begin.

Ceremonial Completion

When you have written the statement(s), create a small ceremony. You can do this alone or witnessed by soul friends (people who will honor you, your journey, and your statement). Stand, light a candle, speak your Legacy Mission Statement aloud. Place the Legacy Mission Statement and your candle together on your evolving altar. Breathe it in.

Find a way to honor these written statements. Remember them. You may want to write them out and decorate and frame them. You may want to find a way to symbolize them in your imagery journal.

STEPPING STONE EIGHT
YOUR GIVEAWAY WORKSHEET
Write Your Personal Legacy Mission Statement

In remembrance of _____, I choose to use my life to _____, to _____, and to _____.

Since I never know when my final moment will be, today I choose to _____, _____, and _____.

I remind myself, today and every day, to _____, _____, and _____.

Today I make this commitment to myself and to those I love: I promise to live with _____, _____, and _____ as my most valued priorities.

STEPPING STONE EIGHT JOURNAL

Explore Your Unique Giveaway

Journaling Preparation Reminders

See chapter 13.

Journaling Tasks

Consider where you might volunteer to carry out your vision. Wonder about where your unique giveaway is most needed.

Write yourself a letter. Tell yourself about you. Speak of your hopes, dreams, and visions. Put the letter in an envelope with your address written on the front. Seal it. Put a stamp on it. Give it to a friend to mail to you in three months (or six, or in one year).

Other Journaling Options

Free-write as desired about this question:
In order to make a difference in what matters most to you, what is being asked of you?

MY JOURNAL

_____

_____

_____

_____

_____

_____

_____

_____

_____

_____

_____

_____

_____

_____

_____

_____

_____

_____

_____

_____

_____

_____

_____

_____

_____

_____

_____

_____

_____

_____

_____

_____

_____

_____

_____

STEPPING STONE EIGHT IMAGERY JOURNAL
Reveal Your Unique Giveaway

Imagery Tasks

Continue using this imagery journal to tell your evolving story. Paste images that show your giveaway. Express any insights or feelings that came up during your journal practice. Explore brand new ways to concretize and embody your Self. Paste images that symbolize who you are now.

Contemplate Spring and Rebirth. Create a collage of your new life. Include any images that symbolize your experiences from soulwork practices here. If your altar is evolving and changing, consider taking a photo and pasting it here.

MY IMAGERY JOURNAL

MY IMAGERY JOURNAL

MY IMAGERY JOURNAL

MY IMAGERY JOURNAL

CARRY ON

Y ou've been working hard on this path to healing and transformation. Each Standing and Stepping Stone has asked you to stretch. You've dived deeper into your loss, your grief, your memories, and your reflections than ever before. You've found wisdom in the trauma you've examined and moved from the winter of your soul into the rebirth that comes with transmuting your losses into legacy. Now the time has come to stand tall with all you've discovered. Let your light shine through, even as you know that, like Persephone, you will face the underworld again.

When you chose to accept and engage with your grief, you grew to know yourself as much more than the tip of an iceberg. Now you are tasked with bringing that hidden-beneath-the-surface underworld, the whole iceberg of you, into intentional everyday living. There is no such thing as ordinary when it comes to leading a conscious life. It's not necessary to make a big splash. What *is* required is for you to embody all that you've learned and all that you've become. It doesn't matter how you choose to carry out your living legacy, only that you *do*, over and over again. Transforming loss is something you will need to do more than once. Because it will revisit. When it does, having said *Yes!* to the transformational path, you will know how to embrace it. You've undoubtedly withstood sometimes oceanic, and at other times quietly humbling, emotions. You know how to weather the passage and find strength of spirit, courage of heart, and capacity for compassion. You've made your trek into the mythological journey of the underworld *and back.* Now it is time to carry on.

My carrying on includes tending Spirit of Resh Foundation and stewarding twenty acres of beauty at the Sanctuary. But lest that sound overly romantic, let me say that, just as it does for you, this means taking care of myriad details of this or that every day. Mowing and weed-whacking five acres of meadow had a learning curve to it. It takes a dedicated vigilance every spring. Coaxing flowers of every color and vegetable harvests for healthy living out of red-clay earth has been far easier to imagine than accomplish. Growing dynamic partnerships to fertilize Resh and bring our mission into actuality has required many meetings (and more miles than I care to remember). Staying tender-hearted in the fullness of an overflowing plate can be challenging. Feeling blessed includes days of feeling cursed. The struggle to stay true to my transformation is part of my humanity. It's part of everyone's. Especially those of us willing to dig deep. Yet I never, ever, want to exchange that wild ride for a perfectly neat and tidy life (if one even exists). However small or large the impact of my personal legacy mission, I am serving my purpose. Just as Aunt Myrtle said, my service is to the rainbow bridge. I understand that now. Some days are hard. Others are incredibly blessed. Whatever questions, tasks, and concerns fill them, they are mine. And that makes them precious.

This intricacy of blessings and curses being woven into one giant tapestry of life will be true for you, too. That is the way of it. Legacy isn't about living perfectly. It's about living fully, knowing that being human comes with a one-hundred-percent mortality rate. The more we come to terms with this, the freer we are to accept the losses that are inherently part of life. Only then can we live the one we are most meant to live. And *that* is legacy. My prayer for you is to know that your life matters. We are alive today. This moment is all we have. And that is a gift, no matter the wrapping. I hope that you treasure its beauty along with its sorrows and translate life's losses into legacy, again and again.

Thank you for reading this book and for traveling this path of Standing and Stepping Stones. It's been my honor to serve your journey.

GRATITUDE

First and forevermore, thank you Seth. None of this would have happened without you. None. Of it. We are meant to be. Enough said. There aren't words, after all. To all the Loss to Legacy, Resh Story Circle, Grief Support Group participants, and Hermitage clients, you've taught me well. Thank you for your trust in me and your courage in taking giant steps on this winding path. Marnie, your belief in me astounds me; thank you for underwriting this project with your heart as well as your checkbook. I am humbled. To the Spirit of Resh Foundation donors and board of directors (you know who you are!), many thanks for sharing the journey with me. Double thanks to proofreaders! To all my Ancestors, especially Lois and Dave, Mom and Dad, you know my heart. It's yours. Sally, the eggs have most definitely hatched. So grateful for you and glad we are in this nest together. Julie and Jodie, partnering with you on the Loss to Legacy curriculum has been one of my great joys here in the Rogue Valley. How did I get so lucky? Twice! To Resh's *people*, past and present, the Judys, Laurel, Megan, Mary Ann, Julian, Patricia, Elizabeth, Michael, Deborah, Heather, both Carolyns, Maria, Susan, Christine, Jen, and Hayriya, your contributions touch my heart and keep me going. Leslie (writeitstrong.com), I couldn't have chosen a more perfect editor. I'm deeply grateful for your tenacity in buffing *Loss to Legacy* to its brightest shine. Christy and Constellation Book Services, your skills of transforming my manuscript from words on a page into a fully fleshed out book go beyond my imagination. Thank you! To all of you readers, thank you for picking up this book. I hope you work all the steps in it until your legacy shines, too.

ABOUT THE AUTHOR

 Lily Myers Kaplan's career has focused on guiding people to build meaning and purpose from the most challenging life circumstances. With thirty years in private practice, Lily draws from studies in mythology, archetypal psychology and her experiences as a program director of a modern day mystery-school and hospice volunteer manager. Using story as a force for healing in her southern Oregon community is Lily's passion. Serving Spirit of Resh Foundation and providing one-on-one retreats at her twenty-acre Sanctuary at Rainbow Ridge is Lily's way of honoring Ancestors, sharing wisdom gained through hardship, and helping others find beauty in the midst of their losses.

Lily can be reached through Spirit of Resh Foundation or SoulWorks:

www.reshfoundation.org

www.aboutsoulworks.com

Made in USA - Kendallville, IN
1226684_9780692529980
01.20.2021 0804